COACHING FOOTBALL'S DOUBLE EAGLE FLEX DEFENSE

Ted Amorosi

COACHES CHOICE™

ISBN: 1-58518-897-2
Library of Congress Control Number: 2004105093
Book layout and diagrams: Deborah Oldenburg
Cover design: Jeanne Hamilton
Front cover photo: Todd Warshaw/Allsport

Coaches Choice
PO Box 1828
Monterey, CA 93942
www.coacheschoice.com

Dedication

I would like to dedicate this book to my wife Casey.
As all coaches know, it is very hard to be a coach without
the love and support of your wife. Casey, I love you.

I would also like to dedicate this book to my parents Ted and Pat Amorosi.
They have been my number one fans all of my life and
God has blessed me to have them in my life.

Acknowledgments

I would like to thank the following people:

My high school coaches Joe Sheaffer and Tommy Meier.

My college coaches Marty Schaetzle and Rocky Rees.

Don Folmar and Four Chapman for giving me my first coaching opportunities.

Jack Bowman for introducing this defense to me.

Coaches Ellerson, Brown, and Fipp at Cal-Poly SLO.

Coaches Tormey and Mills at the University of Nevada-Reno.

Coach Hammerschmidt at St. Mary's College (CA).

The great kids at Canyon HS (CA) for making the Tombstone Defense a lot of fun.

Coaches Eien and Roark for supplying me with playbooks.

Contents

Introduction

What's in This Book for You

- A complete playbook for the double eagle flex defense.
- A numbering system that will enable any coach to create 44 variations of the double eagle flex.
- The assignments and techniques necessary to play 14 variations of both man and zone coverage.
- Four to six stunts that will complement and enhance each pass coverage.
- Specific strategies versus a number of offensive plays that force a defense into assignment football.

The Basics

Strongside/weakside: The strongside is toward the tight end and the weakside is toward the split end. Strong defenders (e.g., strong tackle) are aligned on the tight end side, and weak defenders are aligned on the split end side.

Gap responsibilities will be given the letter designations shown in Diagram Intro-1.

Diagram Intro-1

The *alignment numbering system* is shown in Diagram Intro-2.

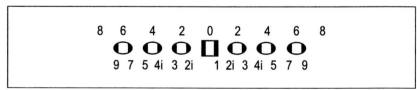

Diagram Intro-2

Receiver Numbers and Formation Names

- **Pro**–Diagram Intro-3A (standard flanker/split end, two-back set).

- **Twin**–Diagram Intro-3B (split end and flanker are aligned on the same side of the formation).

- **Aceback**–Diagram Intro-3C (any offensive set with only one back in the backfield).

- **Doubles**–Diagram Intro-3C (a balanced aceback formation with two receivers on both sides of the center).

- **Trips**–Diagram Intro-3D (an unbalanced aceback formation with three receivers on one side of the center and one receiver on the other side).

- **Empty**–Diagram Intro-3E (an offensive formation with only the quarterback in the backfield).

- **Shotgun**–Diagram Intro-3E (an offensive formation in which the quarterback is not positioned under the center but is catching the back directly from the center. Can also be used with any of the other illustrated formations, not just the empty formation).

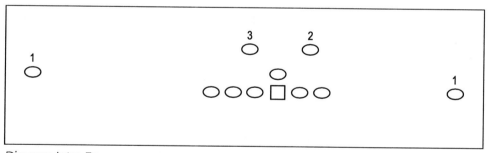

Diagram Intro-3a

Diagram Intro-3b

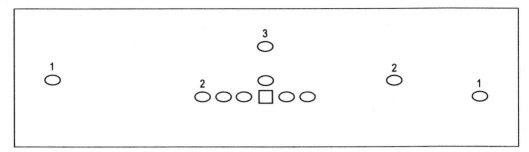

Diagram Intro-3c

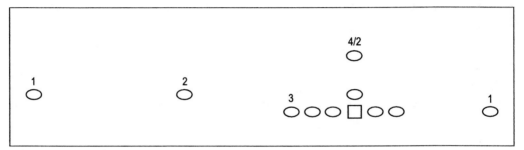

Diagram Intro-3d

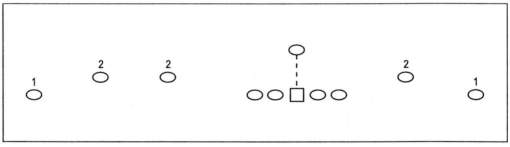

Diagram Intro-3e

History of the Double Eagle Flex Defense

The double eagle flex defense has its roots in the Canadian Football League. Rich Ellerson, currently the head coach at Cal Poly-San Luis Obispo and one of the most brilliant minds in football, was the first person to bring the defense to the United States. He was initially introduced to the system in 1984 when he worked as an assistant for the British Columbia Lions under head coach Don Mathews. After leaving British Columbia in 1986, Ellerson began to expand and mature the system as the defensive coordinator of the Calgary Stampeders.

Ellerson left Canada in 1987 to become an assistant at the University of Hawaii. While at Hawaii, he converted the defense into an 11-man system. When Ellerson joined Dick Tomey's Arizona staff in 1992, he and defensive coordinator Larry McDuff put together an explosive double eagle flex package, cleverly named Desert Swarm, that stymied the best college offenses in the nation.

Credit should also be given to a number of other coaches who were involved in the development and evolution of the double eagle flex. Bob Wagner, Duane Akina, and Marty Long are three outstanding coaches who were instrumental in refining the system.

As this is written, the double eagle flex is currently being run at the college level by the University of Arizona, Cal-Poly San Luis Obispo, the University of Nevada-Reno, and St. Mary's College (CA). It has also become the defense of choice for many successful high school teams across the nation. The vast potential of this extraordinary defense has yet to be fully tapped. Hopefully, this book will not only stimulate thought in the coaching profession, but also be a credit to the pioneers of this innovative system.

Overview of the Double Eagle Flex

The Base Defense

Diagram 1-1 illustrates the base alignment and secondary coverage of the double eagle flex. The base secondary coverage is cover 1. This coverage has five variations. Rover is the adjuster to aceback formations. The following is an overview of the qualifications and techniques for each position.

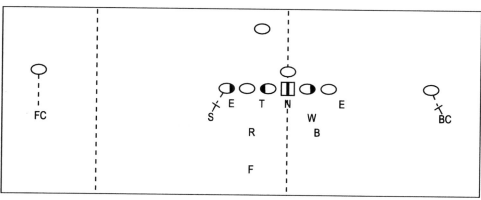

Diagram 1-1

Strong Safety

This player is a hybrid linebacker/defensive back. He lines up in an 8 technique (3 x 3 is normal). If the tight end blocks, he comes up quickly and secures the D gap. Versus pass, he covers the tight end by jamming the tight end and funneling him into the free safety.

Strong End

This defender plays a 7 technique (inside shade of the tight end). His first step should be with his outside foot. He controls the C gap versus run and contains the quarterback versus pass. He must be big and strong enough to defeat the block of the tight end.

Strong Tackle

This defender plays a 3 technique (outside shade of the offensive guard). His first step should be with his inside foot. He controls the B gap. Although size is an asset, quickness is a necessity.

Nose

The nose plays a 0 technique. He is sometimes asked to control both A gaps, but most of the time he will slant into a specific gap. Although some double eagle flex teams prefer to play their nose in a weakside 1 alignment, a slant 0 technique is less predictable and will better enable you to exploit offensive tendencies.

Weak End

He lines up in a ghost 7 technique and employs a jet technique. This player should be the team's best pass rusher. He controls the C gap versus weakside run and collapses the backside (checking cutback) versus strongside run. Versus dropback pass, he is responsible for containing and sacking the quarterback.

Rover

He is a hybrid defensive back/linebacker who lines up five yards deep and slightly inside of the offensive tackle. Versus strongside run, he will shuffle two steps and then scrape outside and assist in containment. If he sees a window as he's scraping, he must plug the gap. Versus weakside run, he will shuffle laterally two steps and then work downhill and check for cutback. Versus pass, he will cover his near back if the formation is a two-back set. Versus an aceback formation, he will adjust to and cover the extra receiver.

Blood

He is the best linebacker on the defense. He lines up five yards deep and slightly inside of the offensive tackle. Versus weakside run, he will shuffle two steps and then scrape outside and contain the play. Versus strongside run, he will shuffle laterally two steps and then work downhill and check for cutback. Versus pass, he will cover his near back.

Whip

He is a hybrid defensive lineman/linebacker who lines up so that his toes are slightly behind the heels of the nose. He must secure the B gap versus weakside run and pursue strongside run from an inside-out position. Versus dropback pass, his assignment will vary depending upon the stunt and coverage. This player is frequently called upon to stunt.

Free Safety

He will line up 8 to 12 yards deep in front of the center (but will cheat to the wide side of the field when the ball is on the hash). He drops to centerfield versus pass. Versus run, he comes up quickly and plays the alley, pursuing the ball from an inside-out position.

Field Corner

He is the team's best cover player. He must cover the #1 receiver aligned to the field with no help from the free safety.

Boundary Corner

He will line up to the short side of the field and cover the #1 receiver. His alignment will be approximately three yards deep and one yard outside of #1. He will jam #1 and funnel this receiver into the free safety.

Advantages of the Double Eagle Flex

- It's a maverick defense. An offense may only face one double eagle flex team in an entire season—often resulting in offensive uncertainty and overly simplified game plans.
- The defense is a multiple eight-man front, which gives it an advantage against the run. Despite this strength, the defense is even better versus the pass. Remember that this defense was originally developed to stop the pass in the Canadian Football League, where teams throw the ball almost every down.

- The defense is a four-level defense. Almost every other defense in football is a three-level defense.
- The defense is sound versus the option; most eight-man fronts are not.
- The defense can remain an eight-man front versus an aceback formation and still retain its ability to play cover 1.
- The defense can easily be converted to a nine-man front versus a two-back formation and still sustain it's ability to play cover 1.
- Pass coverages are easily disguised.
- The defense is conducive to multiple coverages.
- An explosive stunt package (including the zone blitz) can easily be installed into the system.
- The base secondary coverage only requires one island player when the ball is located on the hash (which it is approximately 80 percent of the time). The other pass defenders disrupt the timing of pass routes by jamming receivers and funneling them into the free safety.

2

Coaching Double Eagle Flex Defensive Linemen

Four Cardinal Rules

All defensive linemen have four cardinal rules to follow no matter what is happening in the blocking scheme. These rules are:

- Do not get reached.
- Collapse the backside.
- Wrong-shoulder all kick-out blocks.
- Force double-teams and do not get driven back when they occur.

Each day in practice, every defensive lineman should be drilled in game-like situations that make these four cardinal rules second nature.

7 Technique-Strong End

Stance and Alignment: Three-point stance. Feet parallel or slight stagger of inside foot. Inside shade of tight end (his outside foot pointing at tight end's inside foot).

Responsibilities:

- Run Toward: C gap.
- Run Away: Chase. Defender looks for reverse, counter, cutback.
- Pass: Contain rush.

Keys:

- Primary: Tight end.
- Secondary: Near back, pulling linemen.

Important Techniques: Defender must step with inside foot, get his hands on tight end, and jam the tight end. He must not get driven back or crushed inside.

Key Blocks:

- Tight end blocks 7 technique/inside play: Defender must control the tight end, plug the C gap, and force the play inside.
- Tight end blocks 7 technique/outside play: Defender must control the tight end, work across the tight end's face, and pursue the ball from an inside-out position.
- Tight end releases, tackle turnout block, strongside flow: Defender must use the tackle's body to squeeze play inside, maintain outside leverage, and be prepared for the ballcarrier to bounce the play outside.
- Tight end releases, tackle turnout block, weakside flow: Defender must avoid tackle's block, chase the play as deep as the ball, and check for counter, cutback, and reverse.
- Tight end releases and the near back kicks out the 7 technique: Defender must squeeze the C gap, attack the back with outside forearm, and spill play outside. It is important that the defender does not penetrate across the line of scrimmage and create an alley for the ballcarrier.
- Tight end releases and the near back hook blocks the 7 technique: Defender must first protect the C gap, force the play outside, and pursue the ball from an inside-out position. It is vital that the defender controls the back's outside shoulder.
- Tight end releases and an offensive lineman traps the 7 technique: Defender must attack the blocker on the line of scrimmage with outside forearm and spill play outside.
- Tight end releases/pass: Defender must contain rush.

3 Technique-Strong Tackle

Stance and Alignment: Three- or four-point stance, inside foot back. 3 technique.

Responsibilities:

- Run Toward: B gap.
- Run Away: Squeeze A.
- Pass: B-gap rush.

Keys:

- Primary: Guard, ball movement.
- Secondary: Tackle, pulling linemen.

Important Techniques/Concepts: Defender will employ a jet technique—read on the run. His target is the guard's outside shoulder. His first step is with his inside foot. He must maintain outside leverage, secure the B gap, and not get hooked by the guard.

Key Blocks:

- Guard drive block: Defender must read guard's head, fight pressure, and secure the B gap before pursuing to another area.
- Guard hook block: Defender must maintain outside leverage, keep his shoulders parallel to the line of scrimmage, and plug the B gap.
- Guard turnout block: Defender must squeeze the A gap with the guard's body and look for cutback as he pursues down the line.
- Guard/tackle double-team: Defender must attack the tackle and not get driven back. As a last resort, he should drop his outside hip and roll into and plug the B gap.
- Guard/tackle kiss block: Defender must force a double-team and prevent the tackle from releasing to the next level to block a linebacker.
- Guard/tackle zone: Defender must play it like a hook block.
- Guard blocks inside/tackle cracks: Defender must first jam the guard, fight outside pressure, and flatten across tackle's face.
- Guard blocks inside/tackle cut off: Defender must first jam the guard and prevent the guard from blocking a linebacker. He will then rip through tackle's head and pursue flat along the line of scrimmage.
- Guard blocks inside/no outside pressure: Defender must trap the trapper with an outside forearm and spill the play outside.
- Guard/tackle fold: Defender should penetrate the line of scrimmage if he's beaten tackle's head; otherwise, he should flatten across tackle's face and pursue the ball from an inside-out position.
- Guard pulls outside/no outside pressure: Defender must trap trapper with an outside forearm and spill the play outside.

- Guard pulls inside/tackle cutoff: Defender must get in guard's hip pocket and follow him to the point of attack.
- Guard pulls inside/center blocks the 3 technique: Defender must attack the center, flatten through center's face, and pursue down the line.

0 Technique-Nose

Stance and Alignment: Three- or four-point stance. Minimum to no stagger of the feet. 0 technique, nose to nose with the center.

Responsibilities:

- Run: Playside A gap.
- Pass: Rush either A gap.

Keys:

- Primary: Center, ball movement.
- Secondary: Both guards.

Important Techniques/Concepts:

- Target: Center's facemask.
- Crush technique: Defender will attack center with his hands—inside lockout. He will take a short jab step in the direction of the play, keep his shoulders square to the line of scrimmage, and control both A gaps. It is vital that he remembers that pulling guards indicate point of attack.

Key Blocks:

- Center drive block: Defender will knock the center back. He will stay square, locate ball, and pursue from an inside-out position.
- Center/guard double-team: Defender will attack the guard, stay low, and not get driven back. As a last resort, he will drop his outside hip and roll into and plug the A gap.
- Center hook block: Defender will control center's outside shoulder. He will keep his shoulders parallel to the line of scrimmage and pursue the ball from an inside-out position. It is vital that the nose doesn't get hooked.
- Guard/center zone blocking scheme: Defender will play the center's block like a hook block. It is vital that he jams the center and prevents the center from releasing to the next level to block a linebacker.

- Center blocks away/down block by guard: Defender releases from center and controls outside shoulder of guard.
- Pass: Defender will rush either A gap.

Ghost 7 Technique-Weak End

Stance and Alignment: Two- or three-point stance. Inside foot up. Ghost 7 technique (one to two yards outside of tackle).

Responsibilities:

- Run Toward: C gap.
- Run Away: Chase. Defender will look for reverse, counter, and cutback.
- Pass: Contain rush.

Keys:

- Primary: Tackle, ball movement.
- Secondary: Near back, pulling linemen.

Important Techniques: Defender will employ a jet technique and quickly penetrate the line of scrimmage (one yard) at the snap. He will maintain outside leverage and never get hooked.

Key Blocks:

- Tackle hook block: Defender must beat tackle's head across the line of scrimmage. It is imperative that the tackle is never able to hook the defender.
- Tackle turnout block/weakside flow: Defender will immediately squeeze the B gap. Defender must maintain outside leverage on the play and force the ballcarrier inside. If the play should bounce outside, the defender must be able to react and make the tackle.
- Tackle turnout block/strongside flow: Defender should avoid the tackle's block and chase the play as deep as the ball.
- Tackle blocks inside/pulling lineman blocks defender: This block is a trap or guard-tackle crossblock. Defender must attack the blocker with an outside forearm and spill the play outside.
- Tackle blocks inside/near back blocks the defender: Defender must attack the near back with an outside forearm, stuff the blocker, and force the ballcarrier to bounce the play outside.
- Pass: Defender must contain rush.

Defensive Line Drills

The purpose of all football drills, whether they are for defensive linemen, linebackers, or defensive backs, should be to:

- Enhance athleticism.
- Develop a teaching progression that will create habits that will enable the athlete to perform the basic fundamentals of his position with maximum efficiency.
- Develop the intense level of effort necessary to attain the highest level of success.

Defensive line practices should include the following:

- Movement drills that develop agility, quickness, balance, coordination, and intense effort.
- Tackling drills from different angles.
- Drills that teach the fundamentals of defeating a one-on-one run block (hook, drive, kick-out, trap, etc.).
- Drills that teach the fundamentals of defeating two-on-one run blocks (kiss, fold, zone, double-team, etc.).
- Drills that teach the fundamentals of full- and/or half-line blocking schemes (may or may not include running backs).
- Drills that teach the fundamental skills of defeating a one-on-one pass block (emphasizing specific techniques such as rip under, swim, etc.).
- Drills that teach the skills of slanting, stunting, twisting, etc.
- Game line scrimmages (team, half-line, run hull, etc.).

Coaches who desire a complete package of specific drills should investigate Mark Snyder's excellent book 101 Defensive Line Drills (available from Coaches Choice).

A big question that many double eagle flex coaches need to decide is who will coach the whip. Because this player is a hybrid, he will probably split his time between the defensive line coach (learning run skills) and the linebacker coach (learning pass coverage skills).

3

Coaching Double Eagle Flex Linebackers

Playing linebacker is probably the most demanding and challenging job in football. A linebacker is involved in every aspect of the game. He is expected to play the game from sideline to sideline, and to make tackles with little or no help. Linebackers are expected to be the most aggressive players on the defense, the most ferocious tacklers, the leaders and heart and soul of the entire defense. The concept of being average never occurs to a real linebacker.

A Linebacker's 10 Commandments for Great Run Defense

* Always know the down and distance, formation, and field tendency of your opponent.

* Always gang tackle; never assume that a ballcarrier has been tackled.

* Keep your shoulders parallel to the line of scrimmage for as long as possible; turn and run only as a last resort. Avoid crossing your feet.

* Always pursue relentlessly. Try to keep ballcarriers running laterally and never open up a cutback seam. If you get knocked down, ricochet off the ground and make the tackle.

- Play at one level; avoid lowering and raising your body.

- Always maintain a pad level lower than the blocker and ballcarrier.

- Always take the most direct pursuit angle toward the ballcarrier. Avoid blockers whenever possible, but never take the easy route behind or around a blocker if it takes you out of your path of pursuit.

- Use your hands when taking on a cut block; use your forearm when taking on an isolation block by a running back.

- Don't get tangled up with a blocker. Get separation and ricochet off the block.

- Be aggressive and intimidate your opponent.

A Linebacker's 10 Commandments for Great Pass Defense

- When you recognize pass, sprint to your assigned zone or man.

- Communicate. Be verbal; talk to your teammates.

- If you see the quarterback turn his shoulders to throw, immediately break for his aiming point.

- Attack the ball when it is in the air; catch it at its highest point.

- When attempting an interception, use two hands and remember that you have as much right to the ball as the receiver.

- When playing zone, keep your head on a swivel at all times.

- When playing zone, cover the deepest receiver in your zone and rally up to the short throws.

- When playing zone, force receivers to run a collision course through your zone.

- When covering a running back man-to-man, close the cushion between yourself and the back as soon as possible. Don't give a running back a lot of room to maneuver after a catch.

- Punish receivers if they catch the ball. As you make the tackle, try to rip and strip the ball out of the receiver's possession.

8 Technique-Strong Safety

Stance and Alignment: Two-point stance. Inside foot back. Loose 8 technique (depending upon the down-and-distance situation and offensive tendency, the strong safety may line up anywhere from two to five yards deep/outside of the tight end).

Responsibilities:

- Run Toward: Come up quickly and secure D gap.
- Run Away: Check the tight end first and then pursue.
- Pass: Depends upon stunt and coverage.

Keys:

- Primary: Tight end, ball movement.
- Secondary: Near back, pulling linemen.

Important Techniques: Defender is both a linebacker and defensive back. He must be able to instantly read and react to the tight end's movements. Versus a run in which the tight end blocks the 7 technique, he must close the seam between himself and the tight end and force the ballcarrier to bounce the play outside. When the tight end releases, he must jam the tight end and simultaneously read the near back. If the near back's movements indicate run, the strong safety must constrict the D gap and force the play outside. If the play is pass, his technique will vary depending upon the coverage, but with all variations of the primary coverage (cover 1), the strong safety must be able to jam the tight end and aggressively funnel the tight end into the free safety.

Key Blocks:

- Tight end blocks 7 technique/near back kicks out strong safety: This block is an off-tackle play. Defender must fill tight to tight end's block and seal off any inside seams. He must attack the blocker with outside forearm and spill the play outside.
- Tight end blocks 7 technique/near back hook blocks strong safety: This is a sweep. Defender must keep his shoulders parallel to the line of scrimmage and attack the blocker with an inside forearm. He must force ballcarrier inside or wide and deep.
- Tight end blocks defender/near back blocks 7 technique: This is an off-tackle play. Defender must jam the tight end and use the tight end's body to squeeze the play inside. Defender should maintain outside leverage on the tight end's block and expect ballcarrier to bounce outside.
- Tight end releases/near back doesn't block 7 technique: This is a play-action pass. Defender must jam and cover the tight end and funnel him into the free safety.
- Tight end releases and hook blocks defender: This is a sweep. Defender must defeat the tight end's block and blow the play up in the backfield.
- Tight end releases/flow away: Defender must check tight end first and then pursue checking for counter, reverse, and cutback.
- Tight end releases/near back pass blocks: The play is pass. Defender's reactions and techniques will depend upon coverage.

Rover

Stance and Alignment: Two-point stance. Versus two-back sets, defender will line up five yards deep on the inside eye of the strongside offensive tackle with a slight stagger of his outside foot (versus I backs or backs away, the defender may slide to the outside eye of his near guard). Defender is the adjuster versus aceback sets and will employ the same jam-and-funnel technique as the boundary corner when covering a wide receiver.

Responsibilities Versus Two-Back Sets:

- Run Toward: Scrape outside and contain.
- Run Away: Hit man. Shuffle parallel to the line for two steps and then work downhill, pursuing the ball from an inside-out position.
- Pass: Depends upon stunt and coverage.

Keys:

- Primary: Near guard. Defender must remember that pulling guards take precedence over backfield flow.
- Secondary: Backfield flow.

Important Techniques: Slide parallel to the line of scrimmage two steps before reacting downhill. Maintain outside leverage and attack blockers with inside forearm (use hands versus cut blocks).

Key Reactions:

- Strongside sweep: Defender will slide two steps to his outside as he recognizes the blocking pattern and full-flow action of the backfield. He will then scrape outside and attack the football through the inside number of the ballcarrier.
- Weakside sweep: Defender will slide two steps and then work downhill. He will stay behind the ball and make the tackle from an inside-out position.
- Strongside off-tackle play: Defender will slide two steps to his outside as he recognizes blocking pattern and full-flow action of the backfield. He will then scrape outside, squeeze the play inside, and expect the ballcarrier to bounce the play outside.
- Weakside off-tackle play: Defender will slide two steps and then work downhill. He will stay behind the ball and make the tackle from an inside-out position.
- Strongside dive option: Defender will slide two steps to the outside, scrape downhill, and attack the pitch.
- Weakside dive option: Defender will slide two steps, work downhill, and attack the dive.

- Strongside lead (speed) option: Defender will slide two steps to the outside, scrape downhill, and attack the pitch. If blocked by a lead back, he will attack the blocker with an inside forearm, ricochet off the block, and tackle the ballcarrier.
- Weakside lead (speed) option: Defender will slide two steps, work downhill, and play quarterback first and pitch second. If the ball is pitched, defender will maintain inside leverage on the pitch and expect the ballcarrier to cut back.
- Strongside iso: Defender will slide to the outside, but as he recognizes full-flow iso action, he will attack the lead blocker with an inside forearm, stuff the play, and force the ballcarrier back inside toward the pursuit of the blood backer. It is important that as he attacks the lead blocker, he maintains outside leverage on the play and is able to react outside should the ballcarrier bounce the play outside.
- Weakside iso: Defender will slide two steps, work downhill, and tackle the ballcarrier from an inside-out position.
- Counter action (both running backs go in opposite directions): Defender's first priority is to read the blocking pattern as this will probably lead him to the point of attack. If he is unable to determine the play's direction from the blocking pattern, the defender must stay at home and protect his area first. He must expect that the ballcarrier will bounce the play outside.

Blood Linebacker

Stance and Alignment: Two-point stance. Versus two-back sets, defender will line up five yards deep on the inside eye of the weakside offensive tackle with a slight stagger of his outside foot (versus I backs or backs away, the defender may slide to the outside eye of his near guard). Versus aceback, the defender will move to a middle linebacker position if cover 1 stay or cover 3 is called.

Responsibilities Versus Two-Back Sets:

- Run Toward: Scrape outside and contain.
- Run Away: Hit man. Shuffle parallel to the line for two steps and then work downhill, pursuing the ball from an inside-out position.
- Pass: Depends upon stunt and coverage.

Keys:

- Primary: Near guard. Defender must remember that pulling guards takes precedence over backfield flow.
- Secondary: Backfield flow.

Important Techniques: Slide parallel to the line of scrimmage two steps before reacting downhill. Maintain outside leverage and attack blockers with inside forearm (use hands versus cut blocks).

Key Reactions:

- Weakside sweep: Defender will slide two steps to his outside as he recognizes blocking pattern and full-flow action of the backfield. He will then scrape outside and attack the football through the inside numbers of the ballcarrier.

- Strongside sweep: Defender will slide two steps and then work downhill. He will stay behind the ball and make the tackle from an inside-out position.

- Weakside off-tackle play: Defender will slide two steps to his outside as he recognizes blocking pattern and full-flow action of the backfield. He will then scrape outside, squeeze the play inside, and expect the ballcarrier to bounce the play outside. As he scrapes, the defender must make certain that the lead back blocks the 7 technique. If the lead back releases into the flats instead of blocking, the play is not a run; it is a play-action pass and the defender must cover this back.

- Strongside off-tackle play: Defender will slide two steps and then work downhill. He will stay behind the ball and make the tackle from an inside-out position.

- Weakside dive option: Defender will slide two steps to the outside, scrape downhill, and attack the pitch.

- Strongside dive option: Defender will slide two steps, work downhill, and attack the dive.

- Weakside lead (speed) option: Defender will slide two steps to the outside, scrape downhill, and attack the pitch. If blocked by a lead back, he will attack the blocker with an inside forearm, ricochet off the block, and tackle the ballcarrier.

- Strongside lead (speed) option: Defender will slide two steps, work downhill, and play quarterback first and pitch second. If the ball is pitched, defender will maintain inside leverage on the pitch and expect the ballcarrier to cut back.

- Weakside iso: Defender will slide to the outside, but as he recognizes full-flow iso action, he will attack the lead blocker with an inside forearm, stuff the play, and force the ballcarrier back inside toward the pursuit of rover. It is important that as he attacks the lead blocker, the defender maintains outside leverage on the play and is able to react outside should the ballcarrier bounce the play outside.

- Strongside iso: Defender will slide two steps, work downhill, and tackle the ballcarrier from an inside-out position.

- Counter action (both running backs go in opposite directions): Defender's first priority is to read the blocking pattern, as this will probably lead him to the point of attack. If unable to determine the play's direction from the blocking pattern, the defender must stay at home and protect his area first. He must expect that the ballcarrier will bounce the play outside.

Whip

Stance and Alignment: Two-point stance, outside foot back. 3 technique (outside eye of the offensive guard), one to two feet behind the heels of the nose and weakside end.

Responsibilities:

- Run Toward: B gap.
- Run Away: Pursue ballcarrier from inside-out position if not involved in a stunt.
- Pass: Depends upon stunt and coverage.

Keys:

- Primary: Guard, ball movement.
- Secondary: Tackle.

Important Techniques/Concepts: Defender's target is guard's outside shoulder. His first step is with his inside foot. He must react quickly to guard's block. He can't get knocked backwards and create a bubble or cut off rover or the blood backer. He must maintain outside leverage and can't get hooked. When flow is away, the defender will pursue flat down the line in a good, low hitting position and maintain an inside-out position on the ballcarrier.

Key Blocks:

- Guard drive block: Defender must quickly attack the guard while maintaining outside leverage. He must fight pressure, locate the ball, and quickly pursue the play.
- Guard hook block: Defender must not allow the guard to get his head outside of him; he must maintain outside leverage and plug the B gap.
- Guard/tackle double-team: Defender must attack the tackle. It is imperative that he doesn't get driven back. As a last resort, he should plug the B gap by dropping his outside knee and rolling to his outside.
- Strong zone scheme: Defender must pursue down the line maintaining an inside-out position on the ballcarrier. He will flatten across center's face if nose doesn't do his job and allows center to release to second level.
- Guard blocks inside/tackle cracks: Defender will fight pressure, flatten across tackle's face, and pursue the ball from an inside-out position.
- Guard blocks inside/tackle cut off: Defender must quickly pursue flat down the line and maintain an inside-out position on the ball. He should avoid tackle's block or quickly ricochet off it if engagement should occur.

- Guard blocks inside/near back blocks defender: Defender must close inside and attack the blocker with an outside forearm. He must plug the B gap and force the ballcarrier to bounce outside.
- Guard pulls outside/tackle cracks: Defender should quickly flatten across tackle's face and pursue the play from an inside-out position.
- Guard pulls inside: Defender must quickly pursue down the line and maintain an inside-out position on the ballcarrier.
- Guard pass blocks: Depends upon stunt and coverage called.

Linebacker Drills

The coaching points for developing a defensive line drill program also pertain to linebackers. Linebackers must also be drilled on the fundamental skills of both man and zone coverage. The following are some suggestions for teaching linebackers these skills:

- Drills that teach the specific techniques and body position for covering all of the pass routes that the linebacker will be required to cover (hook, swing, out, etc.).
- One–on-one drills (linebacker versus tight end and running backs).
- Ball-catching drills (often neglected).
- Blitz drills (that emphasize read- and react-on-the-run skills).
- Seven-on-seven drills.
- Full pass hull scrimmages that include draws, screens, play-action passes (with an occasional run thrown in to keep things honest).
- A formation adjustment/front-and-stunt drill.
- A crack-and-replace drill with defensive backs and wide receivers.
- A two-on-two and three-on-three drill that teaches linebackers and defensive backs to deal with picks, rubs, etc.
- Drills that teach defenders to strip the ball out of a receiver's possession.

Coaches desiring a complete repertoire of linebacker drills would do well to investigate Jerry Sandusky's excellent book *101 Linebacker Drills* (available from Coaches Choice).

4

Coaching Double Eagle Flex Secondary Techniques

Cover 1 is the base secondary coverage of the double eagle flex defense. As mentioned in Chapter 1, the defense outlined in this book employs five different variations of this coverage. Although the strengths of this coverage include the ability to disguise each variation and to pressure the quarterback with a number of different pressure packages from each variation, the main strength of the coverage is its ability to jam receivers at the line and disrupt the timing of the opponent's passing game. This chapter will explain the various techniques of this coverage and briefly touch upon some of the drills used to teach these techniques.

The Field Corner

Stance, Alignment, and Responsibility

When the ball is on the hash, the field corner will line up toward the wide side of the field and cover the #1 receiver. He will be approximately seven yards deep and slightly inside of #1. The defender will concentrate on covering #1 and not concern himself with run support unless he is absolutely certain that the ball has crossed the line of scrimmage. The defender's stance should be as follows:

- Narrow base, feet inside of his armpits. Outside foot is up (toe-heel relationship).
- Weight is on his front foot.
- His knees are bent and his hips are lowered.
- His back is slightly rounded with his head and shoulders over his front foot.
- His arms will hang loosely.
- From this stance and alignment, the defender should be able to see both the receiver and quarterback out of his periphery.

Backpedal Technique

- The defender will maintain inside leverage on receiver #1; he should never allow the receiver to get head up with him.
- The field corner will keep a good forward lean as he backpedals.
- He will push off his front foot when the ball is snapped and make his first step with his back foot. He keeps his weight on the balls of his feet.
- As he backpedals, he should reach back with each step and pull his weight over his feet.
- He will keep his feet close to the ground during the backpedal.
- He will take small to medium steps and not overstride.
- His arms will be relaxed and bent at a 90-degree angle, but pumping vigorously.
- The defender will maintain a cushion of approximately three to five yards from the receiver.
- He will keep his shoulders parallel to the line and not let the receiver turn him.
- He will mirror the receiver's movements and keep his outside shoulder on the receiver's inside shoulder.
- It is vital that the defender controls the speed of his backpedal. When the receiver makes his break, the defender must be under control and able to gather and break quickly in the direction of the receiver's break.
- He must concentrate on the base of the receiver's numbers until the receiver makes his final break.
- The defender should anticipate the receiver's break when the receiver changes his forward lean, begins to chop his feet, or widens his base.
- Whenever a receiver gets too close to him, the field corner must turn and run with the receiver, keeping his body between the ball and the receiver.

Plant and Drive

- When the receiver makes his final break, the defender should drop his shoulder in the direction of the receiver's break and explode in that direction. He should quickly close the cushion and make his break parallel to the receiver's break.

- The defender must not lose concentration on the receiver, nor should he look for the ball until he's closed his cushion and he sees the receiver look for the ball.

Playing the Ball

- The defender should attack the ball at its highest point when attempting an interception.

- When the ball is inside of the defender and the receiver is outside of him, the defender should play the ball, not the receiver.

- When the receiver is between the defender and the ball, the defender should play the ball through the receiver's upfield shoulder. He should never cut in front of the receiver to make an interception unless he is absolutely sure that he can get two hands on the ball.

- The defender should try to catch the ball or break up a pass with two hands, not one.

- The defender should always knock the ball toward the ground, never up in the air.

- If the receiver catches the ball, the defender should try to strip it.

- If the defender makes an interception, he should yell "oski" and head toward the nearest sideline.

The Boundary Corner

Stance and Alignment

- When the ball is on the hash, the boundary corner will line up with his nose on the outside eye of receiver #1. His normal depth should be approximately three yards deep, but this depth may vary, from an alignment that crowds the line of scrimmage to one that is five yards deep. The defender's depth will ultimately depend upon his own ability and also the ability of the receiver that he must cover.

- Ideally, the defender's feet should be parallel to the line of scrimmage. A slight toe-instep stagger of the outside foot is also permissible if it feels more comfortable and functional for the defender.

- The defender's weight should be over the balls of his feet, with more emphasis put on the inside foot.

- The defender's eyes should be focused on the midsection of the receiver.

- When the ball is in the center of the field, the boundary corner will assume the same stance, alignment, and techniques as the field corner.

Jam Technique

- The defender will jam the receiver by extending his arms and locking his elbows. Becoming overly aggressive when executing this technique is a mistake because it can cause the defender to lunge and lose his balance, thereby allowing the receiver to easily get open.

- When the receiver comes off the line, the defender will slide laterally in a manner that mirrors the receiver's release.

- The defender will redirect an outside release by jamming the receiver with both hands and forcing him to run horizontally down the line. When the receiver starts to make vertical progress, the defender will immediately roll his hips and snap his head toward the receiver. Although the defender will release his outside hand from the receiver at this point, he will continue to jam with his inside hand. It now becomes crucial that the defender maintains a tight gap between himself and the receiver's back hip as they run down the field.

- When the receiver attempts an inside release, the defender will jam him as far as possible to the inside with his outside hand. The defender will attempt to maintain a position on the receiver's outside shoulder. From this position, he will be able to locate the quarterback through the receiver's body.

The Free Safety

Stance and Alignment

- The free safety lines up 8 to 15 yards deep (depending upon down-and-distance and offensive tendency). Normally, the free safety will line up directly in front of the center, but he may move to the outside shoulder of the offensive tackle (toward the wide side of the field) if the offense splits two or more receivers toward this side of the field.

- It is best that this defender assumes a parallel stance, but a slight stagger is permissible.

- The defender's weight should be on the balls of his feet, with his heels slightly raised off the ground.

- His knees should be bent slightly and his hips should be lowered.
- His waist should also be bent slightly, causing his back to appear slightly rounded.
- His hands and arms should be relaxed and hang loosely.
- He will key the ball and the uncovered linemen.

Techniques and Responsibilities Versus the Pass

- The defender's first three steps are extremely important because they will enable him to read the play and to begin moving toward the best possible position to make a great play. These steps should be made slowly with the defender's shoulders parallel to the line.
- As he reads pass, the free safety should sprint to a position that will place him between the receivers who are being funneled into him. Versus a two-back pro formation, the two receivers will be the tight end and X.
- Provided the quarterback has not finished setting up, the free safety should continue to sprint, keep his head on a swivel, and read the quarterback and receivers. At a depth of approximately 25 yards, the free safety should stop sprinting and resume backpedaling.
- It is vital that the defender stays deeper than any of the receivers who are being funneled into him.
- When the ball is thrown, the free safety will follow the same basic guidelines as the field corner when reacting to the pass.

Techniques and Responsibilities Versus the Run

- The free safety is responsible for providing alley support to all running plays.
- When providing alley support, the defender will go directly to the ball between the primary force player (rover or blood) and the defensive end or strong safety.
- The defender must approach the ballcarrier from an inside-out position and expect that the ballcarrier will cut back.
- Versus option plays, the free safety is responsible for playing quarterback to pitch.
- When confronted by a blocker, it is imperative that the defender protects his legs and prevents the blocker from getting into his body. The defender should try to avoid the blocker if at all possible (without taking himself out of the play). When avoiding the blocker becomes impossible, the defender should become the hammer (not the nail) and punish the blocker.
- Versus the crack block, the defender whose receiver is cracking will give the free safety a "crack-crack" call. The free safety will then attack and/or cover the cracking receiver and the other defender will replace the free safety and support the run.

Cover 1 Funnel and Help Summary

Diagram 4-1 summarizes four field position situations that illustrate which defenders would be funneling which receivers into the free safety. Diagrams 4-1A through 4-1C illustrate three hash situations, and Diagram 4-1D illustrates a situation in which the ball is in the middle of the field.

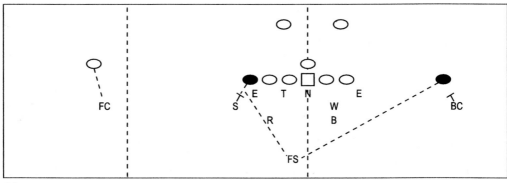

Diagram 4-1a

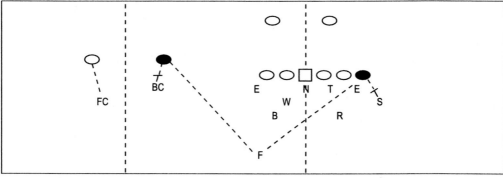

Diagram 4-1b

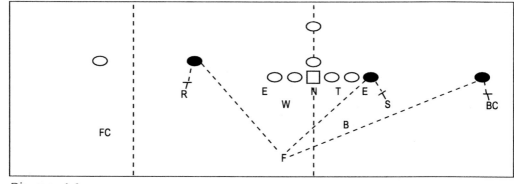

Diagram 4-1c

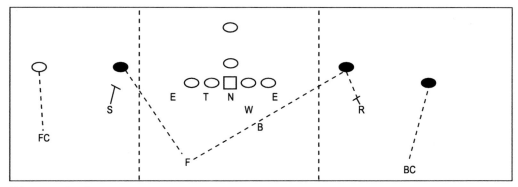

Diagram 4-1d

Defensive Back Drills

Defensive back drills should include:

- Drills that teach tackling skills.

- Drills that teach proper footwork (backpedal, plant, redirect, etc.).

- Jam and funnel drills.

- Ball-catching drills.

- One-on-one drills versus receivers.

- Zone coverage drills that teach quarterback and pattern reads and also emphasize seam coverage situations.

- Crack-and-replace drills with both linebackers and defensive backs.

- Alley support drills for the free safety.

- Drills that teach the exact body position for covering each pass route that a defensive back will encounter (curl, out, comeback, post, post-corner, etc.).

- Two-on-two and three-on-three drills that emphasize picks, rubs, wheels, etc.

- Set adjustment drills that deal with a multitude of different offensive sets (including empty), motions, etc.

Coaches desiring a complete repertoire of defensive back drills should investigate Ron Dickerson's excellent book *101 Defensive Back Drills* (available from Coaches Choice).

5

Cover 1 Variations and Stunts

This chapter will present five variations of cover 1. Four to six stunts that are appropriate for each specific variation will also be illustrated. Obviously, many more stunts could be included with each variation, but it would require another book devoted exclusively to the double eagle flex stunt game.

Diagram 5-1 illustrates the assignments and adjustments of cover 1 versus eight of the most commonly used offensive formations. Note that the standard pro formation has been omitted. The assignments and adjustments for this formation will be presented separately with each specific variation. It should also be mentioned that no coverage assignments will be designated for the running back(s) when the assignments for the pro formation are presented, because these assignments will be predicated upon the specific stunt being employed.

Notice that in Diagrams 5-1D through 5-1H the free safety has moved out of center field and has almost replaced the rover. In this situation, the free safety is playing six to seven yards deep and on the outside shoulder of the offensive tackle. When assuming this position, the free safety will always align on the wide side of the field. Therefore, if the wide side of the field were to the right (rather than the assumed left in Diagram 5-1D), the free safety and blood would switch positions. The reason for aligning the free safety in this position is to stop one of the most explosive plays of the aceback offense—the speed option. From this position, the free safety can not only drop to center field versus the pass, but he can easily scrape outside and stop a speed

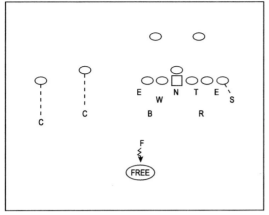

Diagram 5-1a

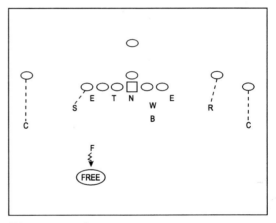

Diagram 5-1b

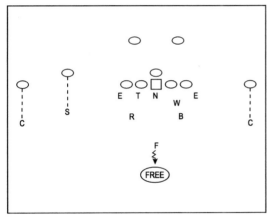

Diagram 5-1c

Diagram 5-1d

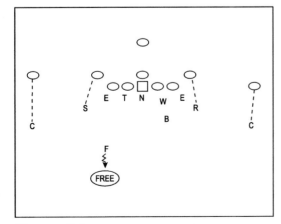

Diagram 5-1e

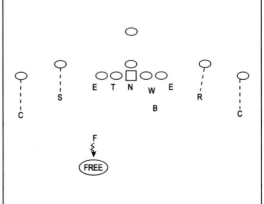

Diagram 5-1f

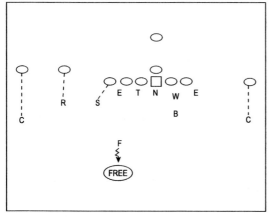
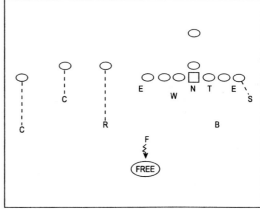

Diagram 5-1g   Diagram 5-1h

option pitch play (the strong safety will play the quarterback). Another advantage of the alignment is that it puts another defender in the box, making it extremely difficult for an aceback offense to run the ball. This alignment is the standard adjustment versus aceback sets for the defense outlined in this book. In an obvious passing situation, or against an opponent with a weak running game, or against an opponent that didn't employ the speed option as part of their package, cover 1 stay might be called. A cover 1 stay call would alert the free safety to align in center field and the blood linebacker to line up in a middle linebacker position.

Cover 1

Cover 1 is the first variation; it is the base. When it is called, the defense will always employ some variation of a five-man pass rush (Diagram 5-2A).

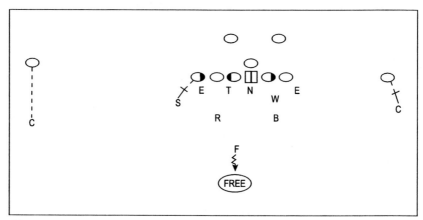

Diagram 5-2a

Cover 1 Stunts

Diagram 5-2B: This is a very basic stunt that involves only one player, the whip linebacker. Whip is attacking the outside shoulder of the guard and controlling the B gap. This stunt requires no adjustments or check-offs versus an aceback set.

Diagram 5-2C: This stunt involves five players. The strong end is slanting inside, attacking the outside shoulder of the offensive tackle and securing the C gap. The strong tackle is slanting across the guard's face and controlling the A gap. Nose is slanting into and controlling the weakside A gap. Whip and the weak end are switching assignments by executing a simple twist. Like the previous stunt, this stunt requires no adjustments or check-offs versus an aceback set.

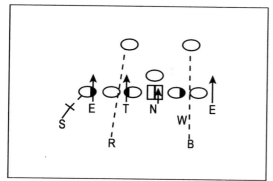

Diagram 5-2b

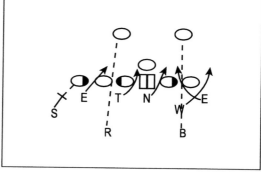

Diagram 5-2c

Diagram 5-2D: This stunt involves four players. The strong safety is creeping toward the line and rushing from the edge. The strong end is locking onto and covering the tight end (obviously, not all teams are blessed with an end who can do this). The nose and whip are playing base technique versus run, but delay stunting into the illustrated gaps versus pass. If the offense does not employ a tight end, the defense will have to check out of the strong safety/strong end aspect of this stunt.

Diagram 5-2E: This stunt illustrates a simple twist between the nose and strong tackle. Blood is blitzing through the weak A gap and whip is creeping toward the line and "selling blitz." As the ball is snapped, whip is pretending to rush in an attempt to draw the weakside guard's block. If the near back releases for a pass, whip must immediately ricochet off the guard's block and cover the back. If the near back continues to block, whip will continue "pretending to rush." The defense does not have to check out of this stunt versus an aceback set.

Diagram 5-2F: This stunt involves only two players. Whip is attacking the outside shoulder of the guard and securing the B gap. Blood is attacking the tackle's outside shoulder, securing the C gap versus run, and spying the near back versus pass. Against an aceback set, the defense will probably want to check out of this stunt.

Diagram 5-2G: This stunt involves five players. The strong safety is creeping toward the line and rushing from the edge. The strong end is locking onto and covering the tight end. Nose is stunting into the weak A gap, and blood is stunting into the strong A gap. Whip is creeping toward the line, "selling blitz," securing the B gap versus run, and spying the near back versus pass. If the offense does not employ a tight end, the defense will have to check out of the strong safety/strong end aspect of this stunt.

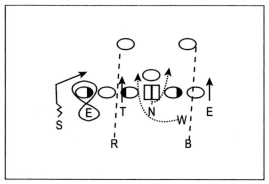

Diagram 5-2d

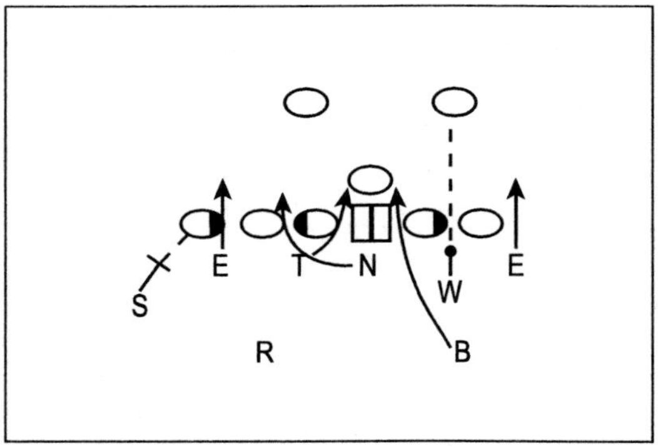

Diagram 5-2e

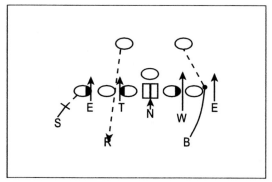

Diagram 5-2f

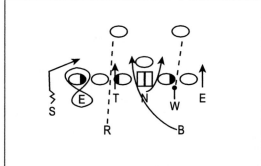

Diagram 5-2g

Cover 1 Rob

The adjustments and assignments for 1 rob (Diagram 5-3A) are identical to cover 1. The advantage of this variation of cover 1 is that it provides the defense with an extra coverage player who will drop into the hole and help either the strong safety or blood with crossing patterns. The disadvantage is that it only provides the defense with a four-man pass rush.

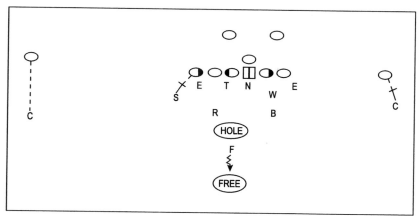

Diagram 5-3a

1 Rob Stunts

Diagram 5-3B: This stunt involves only the nose, who is slanting into the weak A gap. Versus run, whip and blood are playing base technique. Versus pass, whip is spying the near back and blood is dropping to the hole. No checks are necessary versus an aceback formation.

Diagram 5-3C: The strong end is locking onto the tight end and the strong safety is rushing from the edge. Nose is slanting into the weak A gap. Both whip and blood will be playing base technique versus run. Versus pass, blood is covering the near back, and whip is dropping to the hole. If the offense doesn't employ a tight end, the defense will have to check out of the strong safety blitz.

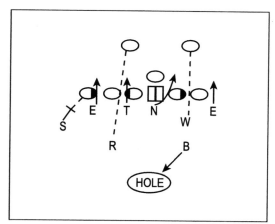

Diagram 5-3b

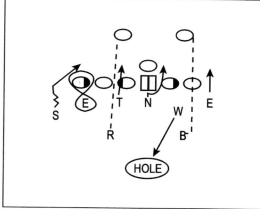

Diagram 5-3c

Diagram 5-3D: This stunt features a weakside line slant. Whip and blood are playing base technique versus run. Versus pass, blood is dropping to the hole, and whip is covering the near back. No check-offs are necessary versus aceback sets.

Diagram 5-3E: This stunt involves four players. The strong end is locking onto the tight end and the strong safety is rushing from the edge (must be checked off if no tight end). The strong tackle and nose are employing base techniques versus run but executing a delayed twist versus pass. Both whip and blood are playing base technique versus run. Whip is dropping to the hole and blood is covering the near back versus pass. This stunt is a good one to use versus an aceback set that employs a tight end.

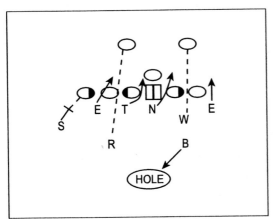

Diagram 5-3d 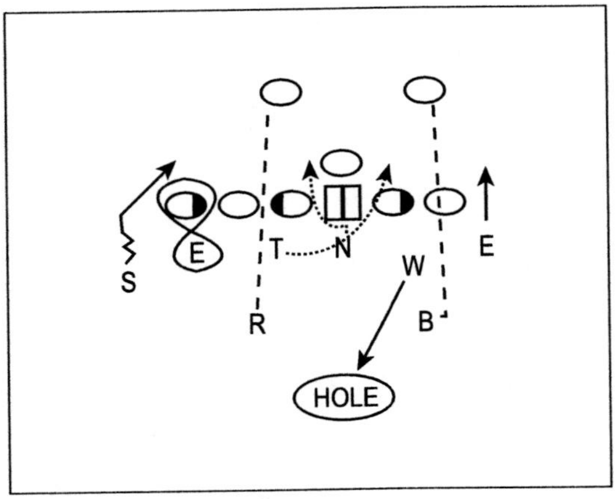   Diagram 5-3e

Cover 1 Rover

The variation 1 rover (Diagram 5-4a) provides the defense with two big advantages: a five-man pass rush and excellent strongside pressure from the edge. The difference between 1 rover and cover 1 is that in 1 rover, the strong safety will be involved in a stunt and the rover will cover the tight end. When confronted by an offensive set that doesn't employ a tight end, the defense will check off to a similar cover 1 stunt.

1 Rover Stunts

Diagram 5-4B: The strong safety is creeping toward the line during cadence and rushing from the edge. The strong end is attacking the near shoulder of the tackle, securing the C gap versus run, and spying the near back versus pass. Whip is attacking the outside shoulder of the guard and controlling the B gap. No check-offs are necessary versus aceback sets that feature a tight end.

Diagram 5-4C: This is a great stunt versus the pass, but weak against the run. Nose is slanting into the weak A gap, and blood is blitzing through the strong A gap. Whip is creeping toward the line, "selling blitz," securing the B gap, and spying the near back. The strong safety is rushing from the edge, containing the quarterback and strongside run and chasing weakside run. The strong end is attacking the near shoulder of the tackle, securing the C gap, and spying the near back. No check-offs are necessary versus aceback sets that feature a tight end.

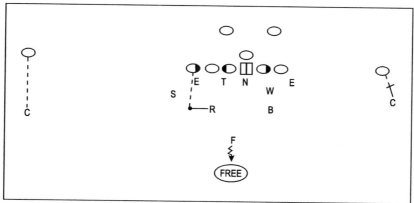

Diagram 5-4a

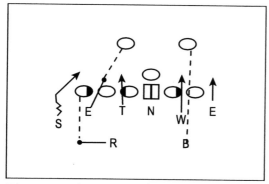

Diagram 5-4b

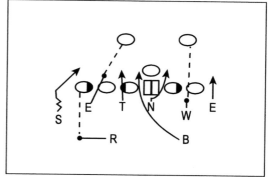

Diagram 5-4c

Diagram 5-4D: This is another great stunt versus the pass, but weak against the run. The strong end, strong tackle, and nose are all slanting weak. Blood is blitzing the strong B gap. Whip is pretending to blitz through the outside shoulder of the guard, securing the B gap versus run, and spying the near back versus pass. The strong safety is rushing from the edge, containing strongside run, chasing weakside run, and spying the near back versus pass. No check-offs are necessary versus aceback sets that feature a tight end.

Diagram 5-4E: This is a good stunt versus both run and pass. The strong end is slanting across the tight end's face, containing strongside runs, and spying the near back versus pass. The strong safety is blitzing through the outside shoulder of the tackle, controlling the C gap, and containing the quarterback. Blood is playing base technique versus run and covering the near back versus pass. Both the nose and whip are playing base technique versus run. Versus pass, these two players will execute a delayed twist. No check-offs are necessary versus aceback sets that feature a tight end.

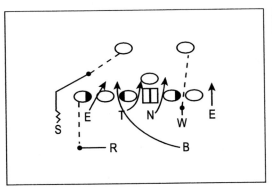

Diagram 5-4d

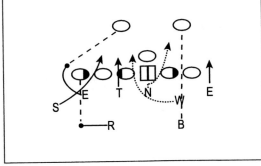

Diagram 5-4e

Diagram 5-4F: This is another good stunt versus both run and pass. The strong safety is rushing from the edge, containing strong run, chasing weak run, and spying the near back. The strong end is attacking the near shoulder of the tackle, securing the C gap, and containing the quarterback. Whip is playing base technique versus run and covering the near back versus pass. Both the nose and blood are playing base technique versus run, but against pass, blood will delay blitz through the weak A gap, and nose will delay slant behind the strong tackle through the strong B gap. No check-offs are necessary versus aceback sets that feature a tight end.

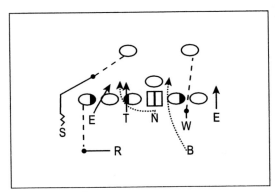

Diagram 5-4f

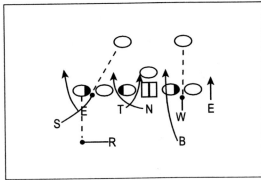

Diagram 5-4g

Diagram 5-4G: This is a good stunt versus pass but weak against run. The strong end is slanting across the tight end's face and containing both the quarterback and strongside run. The strong safety is faking a blitz through the C gap; he will secure this gap versus run and spy the near back versus pass. The strong tackle and nose are twisting and blood is blitzing through the weak A gap at the snap of the ball. During cadence, whip is creeping toward the line, "selling blitz," securing the B gap versus run, and spying the near back versus pass. No check-offs are necessary versus aceback sets that feature a tight end.

Rover–Rob-1 Coverage

Rover-rob-1 (Diagram 5-5A) provides the defense with excellent strongside edge pressure and an extra coverage player to drop to the hole and "rob" crossing routes. Like 1 rover, rover-rob-1 requires the rover to cover the tight end, but leaves the strong safety free to blitz or spy. When confronted by an offensive set that doesn't employ a tight end, the defense should check to a similar 1 rob stunt.

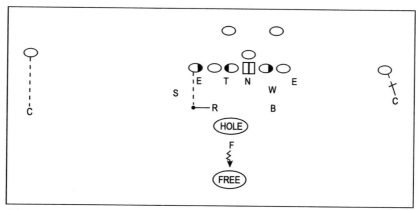

Diagram 5-5a

Rover-Rob-1 Stunts

Diagram 5-5B: This is an excellent stunt versus both run and pass. The strong safety is rushing from the edge and spying the near back. The strong end is attacking the near shoulder of the tackle, securing the C gap, and containing the quarterback. Whip is creeping toward the line, "selling blitz," securing the B gap, and spying the near back. Nose is playing base technique versus run and rushing through the weak A gap versus pass. Blood is playing base technique versus run and dropping to the hole versus pass. No check-offs are necessary versus aceback sets that feature a tight end.

Diagram 5-5C: This is another excellent stunt versus both run and pass. The strong safety is creeping toward the line during cadence and rushing from the edge. The strong end is attacking the near shoulder of the tackle, securing the C gap, and spying the near back. The strong tackle and nose are twisting at the snap of the ball, and both blood and whip are playing base technique versus run. Versus pass, blood will cover the near back and whip will drop to the hole. No check-offs are necessary versus aceback sets that feature a tight end.

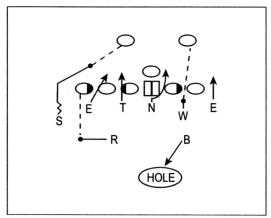

Diagram 5-5b

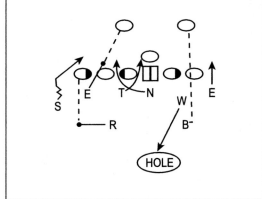

Diagram 5-5c

Diagram 5-5D: The strong end is slanting across the tight end's face, containing strongside runs and spying the near back. The strong safety is blitzing through the outside shoulder of the tackle, controlling the C gap, and containing the quarterback. Nose is slanting into the weak A gap, and whip and blood are playing base technique versus run. Blood is dropping to the hole, and whip is covering the near back versus pass. This stunt is also good versus both run and pass. No check-offs are necessary versus aceback sets that feature a tight end.

Diagram 5-5E: The strong end is slanting across the tight end's face, containing strongside runs and spying the near back. The strong safety is blitzing through the outside shoulder of the tackle, controlling the C gap, and containing the quarterback. Nose is playing base technique versus run and executing a delayed slant behind the strong tackle versus pass. Whip and blood are playing base technique versus run. Whip is dropping to the hole, and blood is covering the near back versus pass. No check-offs are necessary versus aceback sets that feature a tight end.

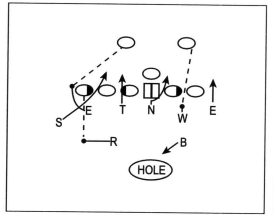

Diagram 5-5d

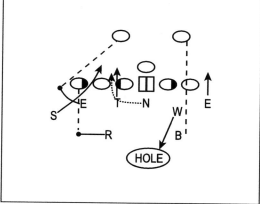

Diagram 5-5e

Fire Zone-1 Coverage

The fire zone blitz is a new and exciting innovation that is easily adaptable to the double eagle flex. When executing this tactic, three defenders will drop to the three areas illustrated in Diagram 5-6A and combo cover the tight end and both running backs. The players dropping into these areas can be either linemen or linebackers. Not all teams are blessed with four defensive linemen who can drop into coverage, but many teams have one or two players who can do this. Many effective fire zone schemes can be devised for these one or two players. Entire books have been written about the fire zone blitz. Space does not permit a complete explanation of this subject in this book. Coaches desiring a complete understanding of the fire zone blitz should investigate Leo Hand's book *101 Fire Zone Blitzes* (available from Coaches Choice).

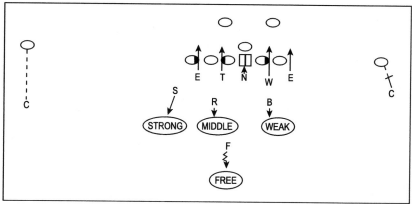

Diagram 5-6a

Fire Zone-1 Stunts

Diagram 5-6B: This stunt pressures the weakside of the offensive formation. Whip is blitzing through the B gap, and blood is blitzing the C gap. The strong safety, rover, and nose are playing base technique versus run and dropping to their respective zones versus pass.

Diagram 5-6C: This is a great stunt versus pass and run. Rover is twisting with the strong end, and whip is twisting with the weak end. The strong safety, nose, and blood are playing base technique versus run and dropping to their respective zones versus pass.

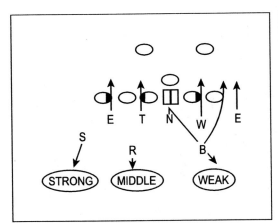

Diagram 5-6b

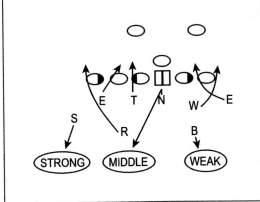

Diagram 5-6c

Diagram 5-6D: The strong safety is creeping toward the line during cadence and blitzing from the edge. Nose and whip are employing base reads versus run and executing a delayed twist versus pass. The strong end, rover, and blood are playing base techniques versus run and dropping into their respective zones versus pass.

Diagram 5-6E: This is an excellent stunt versus pass. Rover is blitzing through the strong A gap, and whip and the weak end are twisting as the ball is snapped. The strong safety, nose, and blood are employing base technique versus run and dropping to their respective zones versus pass.

Diagram 5-6F: This is another great stunt versus pass. The strong safety and strong end are twisting at the snap. Except for two shuffle steps to the outside at the snap, rover is playing the run as usual. Versus pass, rover will drop to the strong zone. Whip is blitzing the B gap and blood is blitzing the C gap. The weak end and nose are employing base techniques versus run and dropping to their respective zones versus pass.

Diagram 5-6G: Both blood and rover are blitzing through the A gaps. Whip is creeping toward the line during cadence, "selling blitz," securing the B gap versus run, and dropping to the weak zone versus pass. The strong safety and strong tackle are employing base techniques versus run and dropping to their respective zones versus pass.

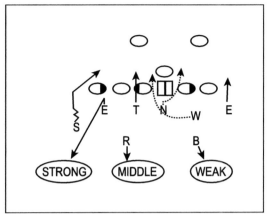

Diagram 5-6d

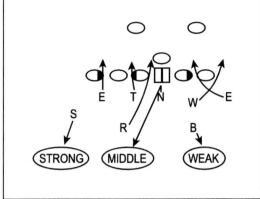

Diagram 5-6e

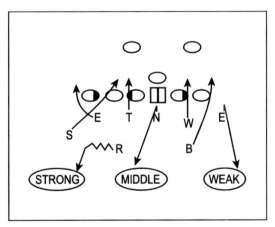

Diagram 5-6f

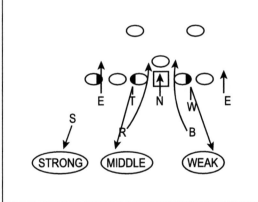

Diagram 5-6g

6

Zero Coverage
Variations and Stunts

Zero coverage is a man-man coverage that doesn't employ a free safety. The strength of zero coverage is that it has eight or nine defenders in the vicinity of the box attacking the gaps and penetrating the line of scrimmage. Its weakness is that all secondary defenders are locked on receivers and none are keying the ball. Therefore, if a run breaks the line of scrimmage or a defensive back gets beat deep, a good chance exists that a touchdown will result. Despite its weakness, zero coverage can cause an offense a lot of problems and has the potential to produce some great defensive plays.

This chapter will present seven variations of zero coverage. The first variation is called Z-F (because the free safety is involved in covering a primary receiver—usually the tight end). Z-F is the base zero coverage. The assignments and adjustments for Z-F are illustrated in Diagram 6-1.

All seven variations of zero coverage will require the boundary corner to play the same technique as the field corner (inside leverage, seven yards off, etc.). When playing this technique, the boundary corner should disguise his intentions. The free safety should also disguise his intentions by lining up in one position and stemming to another during cadence.

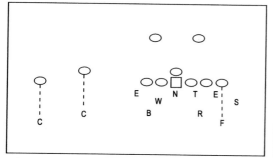

Diagram 6-1a

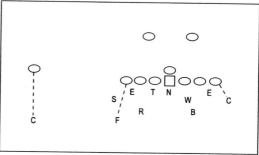

Diagram 6-1b

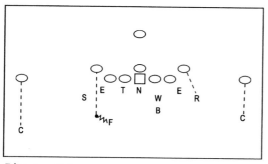

Diagram 6-1c

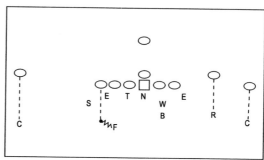

Diagram 6-1d

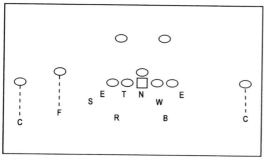

Diagram 6-1e

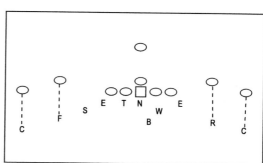

Diagram 6-1f

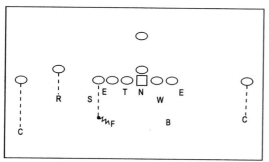

Diagram 6-1g

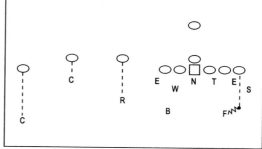

Diagram 6-1h

Z-F Coverage

This variation provides the defense with a six-man pass rush. Rover will make all adjustments to aceback formations (Diagram 6-2A).

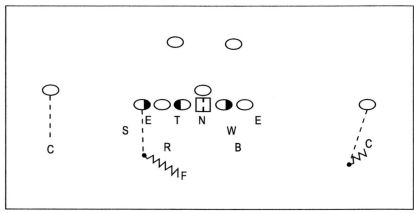

Diagram 6-2a

Z-F Stunts

Diagram 6-2B: This is a good stunt versus run because it leaves blood and rover free to pursue the ball. The strong safety is creeping toward the line during cadence, rushing from the edge, containing the quarterback and strongside run, and chasing weakside run. The strong end, strong tackle, and nose are slanting toward the weakside and the whip is blitzing the B gap. Because rover is not involved in a stunt, no check-offs are necessary versus aceback sets.

Diagram 6-2C: The strong safety is rushing from the edge, and the strong end is attacking the near shoulder of the offensive tackle, securing the C gap, and spying the near back. Nose is slanting weak and rover is blitzing the strong A gap. Whip and the weak end are twisting. Blood is playing base technique versus run and covering the near back versus pass. Because rover is involved in a blitz, the defense must either check out of this stunt or continue with it sans the rover blitz versus aceback sets.

Diagram 6-2D: This is a good stunt versus pass. The strong safety is rushing from the edge, and the strong end is attacking the near shoulder of the offensive tackle, securing the C gap, and spying the near back. The strong tackle and nose are slanting weak and rover is blitzing the strong B gap. Whip is creeping toward the line, "selling blitz," securing the B gap, and spying the near back. Blood is blitzing the C gap. The defense must check out of this stunt versus aceback sets.

Diagram 6-2E: The strong end is slanting across the tight end's face, securing the D gap and spying the near back. The strong safety is blitzing the C gap, and rover is blitzing the B gap. The strong tackle and nose are slanting weak, and whip is blitzing the B gap. Blood is playing base technique versus run and covering the near back versus pass. Because the strong A gap will be left unguarded when rover adjusts to aceback sets, it is best to check out of this stunt in this situation.

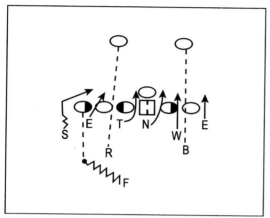

Diagram 6-2b

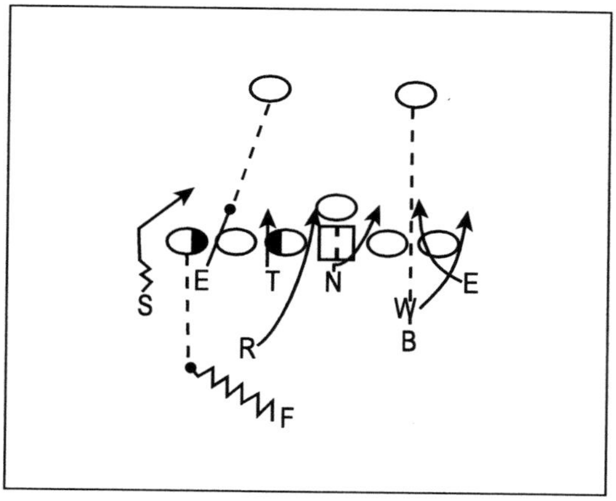

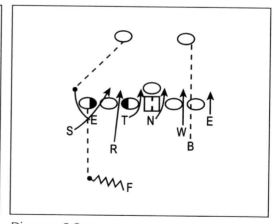

Diagram 6-2c

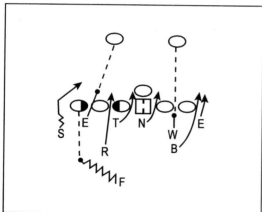

Diagram 6-2d

Diagram 6-2e

Diagram 6-2F: This is another good run stunt that leaves the rover and blood free to pursue the ball. The strong end is slanting across the tight end's face, securing the D gap, and the strong safety is blitzing the C gap. Rover and blood are playing base technique versus run and covering the near back versus pass, and whip is blitzing the B gap. Nose is playing base technique versus run and delay rushing behind the strong tackle through the B gap versus pass. This stunt requires no check-offs versus aceback sets.

Diagram 6-2G: This is another good run stunt. The strong safety is creeping toward the line during cadence and rushing from the edge, and the strong end is attacking the shoulder of the tackle and securing the C gap. Whip and the weak end are twisting, and blood and rover are playing base techniques versus run and covering the near back versus pass. Nose is playing base technique versus run and delay rushing behind the weak end versus pass. This stunt requires no check-offs versus aceback sets.

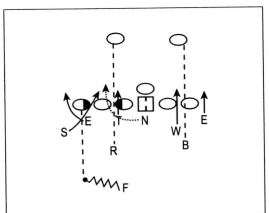

Diagram 6-2f

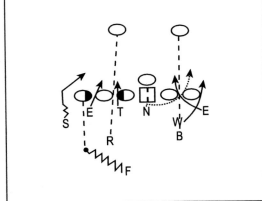

Diagram 6-2g

Z-R Strong Coverage

This variation also provides the defense with a six-man pass rush (Diagram 6-3A). All Z-R strong stunts illustrated in this section are good stunts versus offensive sets that employ a tight end. The defense should check to a similar variation of a Z-F stunt versus sets that don't employ a tight end. Because the free safety becomes the adjuster versus aceback sets, all of these stunts are also good versus any aceback set that employs a tight end.

Z-R Strong Stunts

Diagram 6-3B: This is a good run stunt. The strong safety is creeping toward the line during cadence and rushing from the edge, and the strong end is attacking the shoulder of the tackle and securing the C gap. Whip is blitzing the B gap, and blood is playing base technique versus run and covering the near back versus pass.

Diagram 6-3C: This stunt is good versus pass. The strong safety is creeping toward the line during cadence and rushing from the edge, and the strong end is attacking the

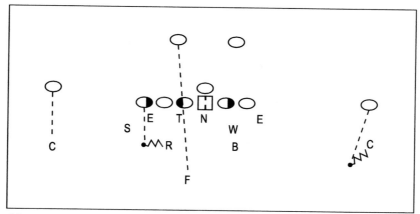

Diagram 6-3a

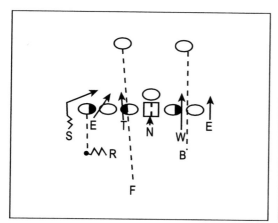

Diagram 6-3b

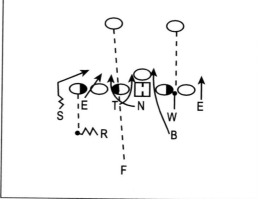

Diagram 6-3c

shoulder of the tackle and securing the C gap. The strong tackle and nose are twisting, and blood is blitzing through the weak A gap. Whip is creeping toward the line during cadence, "selling blitz," securing the B gap, and spying the near back.

Diagram 6-3D: This is a good run stunt. The strong safety is creeping toward the line during cadence and rushing from the edge, and the strong end is attacking the shoulder of the tackle and securing the C gap. Whip is twisting with the weak end, and blood is playing base technique versus run and covering the near back versus pass.

Diagram 6-3E: This is a good run stunt. The strong end is slanting across the tight end's face, securing the D gap, and the strong safety is blitzing the C gap. Blood is playing base technique versus run and covering the near back versus pass, and whip is blitzing the B gap. Nose is playing base technique versus run and delay rushing behind the strong tackle through the B gap versus pass.

Diagram 6-3F: This is another good pass stunt. The strong end is slanting across the tight end's face, securing the D gap, and the strong safety is blitzing through the C gap. The weak end is attacking the near shoulder of the offensive tackle and securing the C gap. Blood is scraping outside and containing the quarterback and weakside run. Whip is creeping toward the line during cadence, "selling blitz," securing the B gap, and spying the near back.

Diagram 6-3G: This is a good stunt versus both pass and run. The strong end is slanting across the tight end's face, securing the D gap, and the strong safety is blitzing through the C gap. The strong tackle and nose are slanting weak. The free safety is checking the strong B gap for run and covering the near back versus pass. The weak end and whip are twisting, and blood is playing base technique versus pass and covering the near back versus pass.

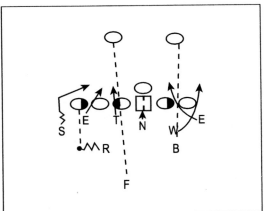

Diagram 6-3d

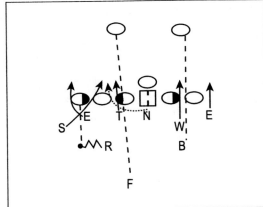

Diagram 6-3e

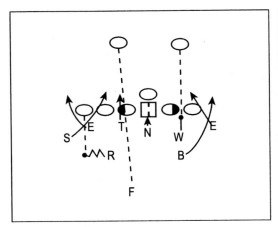

Diagram 6-3f

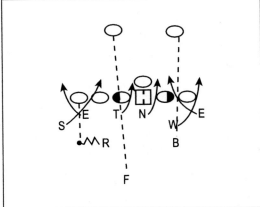

Diagram 6-3g

Z-R Weak Coverage

The same coaching points that were noted for Z-R strong coverage also apply to this coverage (Diagram 6-4A).

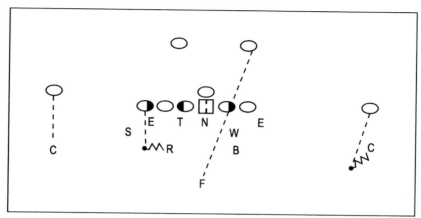

Diagram 6-4a

Z-R Weak Stunts

Diagram 6-4B: This is a good stunt versus pass and run. The strong safety is rushing from the edge, and the strong end is attacking the shoulder of the tackle, securing the C gap, and spying the near back. Nose is slanting into the weak A gap. Whip is blitzing through the strong A gap, and blood is blitzing the weak B gap. Whenever any Z-R weak stunt is used, the free safety not only covers the weak back, but also scrapes outside and contains weakside run. Versus strongside run, he works downhill and checks cutback.

Diagram 6-4C: This is also a good stunt versus pass and run. The strong safety is creeping toward the line during cadence, rushing from the edge; he will contain strongside run and chase weakside run. Versus pass, he will spy the near back. The strong end is attacking the shoulder of the tackle and securing the C gap. Nose is slanting into the strong A gap and blood is blitzing through the weak A gap. Whip is blitzing through the B gap.

Diagram 6-4D: This is another good stunt versus pass and run. The strong safety is rushing from the edge, and the strong end is attacking the shoulder of the tackle, securing the C gap, and spying the near back. Whip is creeping toward the line during cadence and blitzing through the B gap. It is vital that whip gains quick penetration of the gap. Blood is blitzing through the outside shoulder of the offensive tackle. Nose is playing base technique versus run and executing a delayed blitz through the weak B gap versus pass.

Diagram 6-4E: This is a good run or pass stunt. The strong end is slanting across the tight end's face, securing the D gap, and spying the near back. The strong safety is blitzing through the C gap, and blood is blitzing through the strong A gap. Nose is slanting weak and the whip and weak end are twisting.

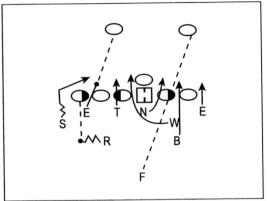

Diagram 6-4b

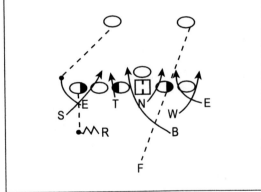

Diagram 6-4c

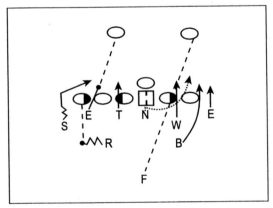

Diagram 6-4d

Diagram 6-4e

Diagram 6-4F: This is a good pass or run stunt. The strong end is slanting across the tight end's face, securing the D gap, and spying the near back. The strong safety is blitzing the C gap, and the strong tackle and nose are slanting weak. Whip is blitzing through the strong B gap, and blood is blitzing through the weak B gap.

Diagram 6-4G: This is a good run or pass stunt. The strong end is slanting across the tight end's face, securing the D gap, and spying the near back. The strong safety is blitzing the C gap. Blood is blitzing through the weak A gap, whip is blitzing through the weak B gap, and both the strong tackle and nose are slanting strong.

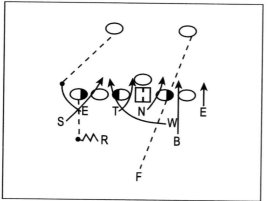

Diagram 6-4f

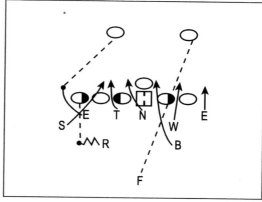

Diagram 6-4g

Z-R Flash Coverage

Z-R flash stunts (Diagram 6-5A) are only usable versus offensive sets that employ a tight end. Versus offensive sets that do not employ a tight end or against aceback sets, the defense should check out of a Z-R flash stunt and into the similar Z-S flash stunt.

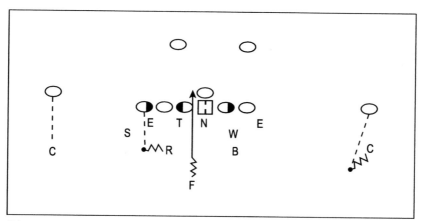

Diagram 6-5a

Z-R Flash Stunts

Diagram 6-5B: This is a good stunt versus run. The strong safety is rushing from the edge and the strong end is attacking the near shoulder of the tackle, securing the C gap, and spying the near back. Nose is slanting into the weak A gap, and the free safety is blitzing through the strongside A gap. Whip is blitzing through the B gap, and blood is playing base technique versus run and covering the near back versus pass.

Diagram 6-5C: This is a good stunt versus pass. The strong safety is creeping toward the line during cadence, rushing from the edge, containing strongside run, chasing weakside run, and spying the near back. The strong end is attacking the shoulder of the tackle and securing the C gap. Nose is attacking the center and attempting to prevent the center from blocking either the free safety or blood, both of whom are blitzing the A gaps. Whip is creeping toward the line during cadence, securing the B gap versus run, and spying the near back versus pass.

Diagram 6-5D: This is a good run or pass stunt. The strong end is slanting across the tight end's face, securing the D gap, and spying the near back. The strong safety is blitzing the C gap, and the free safety is blitzing the B gap. The weak end and whip are twisting. Blood is playing base technique versus run and covering the near back versus pass.

Diagram 6-5E: This is a good stunt versus pass. The strong end is slanting across the tight end's face, securing the D gap, and spying the near back. The strong safety is blitzing the C gap. The free safety and blood are blitzing the A gaps, and whip is creeping toward the line during cadence, "selling blitz," securing the B gap versus run, and spying the near back versus pass.

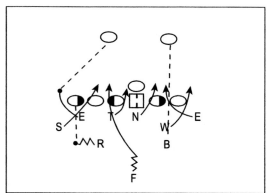

Diagram 6-5b

Diagram 6-5c

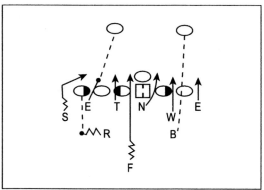

Diagram 6-5d

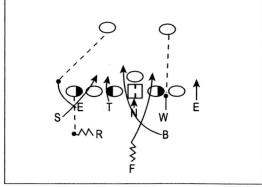

Diagram 6-5e

Z-S Strong Coverage

This variation (Diagram 6-6A) also provides the defense with a six-man pass rush. All Z-S strong stunts illustrated in this section are good stunts versus any offensive sets. The free safety becomes the adjuster versus aceback sets.

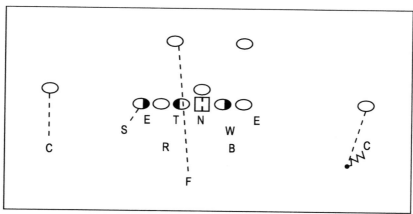

Diagram 6-6a

Z-S Strong Stunts

Diagram 6-6B: This is a good stunt versus the pass and weakside run. Rover is blitzing the strong A gap, nose is slanting into the weak A gap, whip is blitzing the B gap, and blood is playing base technique versus run and covering the near back versus pass.

Diagram 6-6C: This is a good stunt versus both run and pass. The strong end is attacking the near shoulder of the offensive tackle and securing the C gap. Rover is blitzing through the outside shoulder of the tight end and containing the quarterback and strongside run. The weak end and whip are twisting. Blood is playing base technique versus run and covering the near back versus pass.

Diagram 6-6D: This is a good stunt versus the pass and weakside run. Nose is slanting through the strong A gap, and rover is blitzing the weak A gap. Whip is creeping toward the line during cadence and blitzing through the outside shoulder of the offensive guard. Blood is playing base technique versus run and covering the near back versus pass.

Diagram 6-6E: This is a good stunt versus pass and run. The strong tackle and nose are slanting weak, and rover is blitzing through the outside shoulder of the offensive guard. Blood is playing base technique versus run and covering the near back versus pass. Whip is playing base technique versus run and delay blitzing through the strongside A gap versus pass.

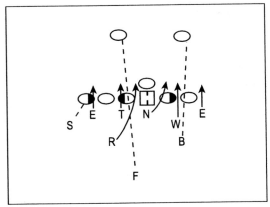

Diagram 6-6b

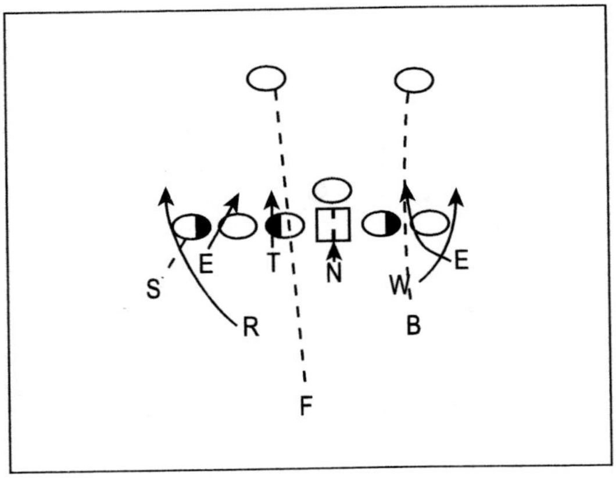

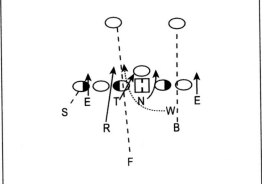

Diagram 6-6c

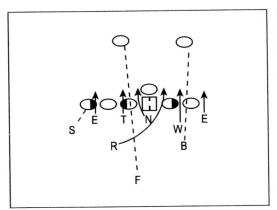

Diagram 6-6d

Diagram 6-6e

Diagram 6-6F: This is a good stunt versus pass and strongside run but weak against weakside run. The strong end is attacking the near shoulder of the offensive tackle and securing the C gap. Rover is blitzing through the outside shoulder of the tight end and containing the quarterback and strongside run. Whip is creeping toward the line during cadence, "selling blitz," securing the B gap versus run, and spying the near back versus pass. Blood is blitzing through the inside shoulder of the offensive guard, and securing the weak A gap. Nose is securing the strongside A gap versus run and delay twisting through the strongside B gap versus pass.

Diagram 6-6G: This is a good stunt versus both pass and run. The strong end is attacking the near shoulder of the offensive tackle and securing the C gap. Rover is blitzing through the outside shoulder of the tight end and containing the quarterback and strongside run. The strong tackle and nose are playing base technique versus run and delay twisting versus pass. Whip is blitzing through the B gap, and blood is playing base technique versus run and covering the near back versus pass.

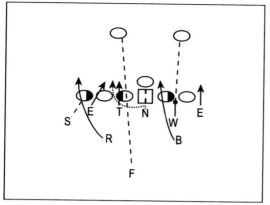

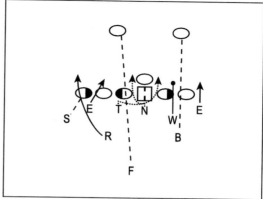

Diagram 6-6f

Diagram 6-6g

Z-S Weak Coverage

The free safety is covering the weak back versus pass, playing the alley versus strongside run, and scraping outside and containing weakside run. All of the other coaching points for Z-S strong also apply to Z-S weak (Diagram 6-7A).

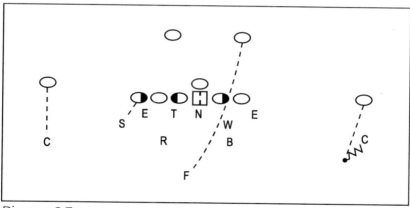

Diagram 6-7a

Z-S Weak Stunts

Diagram 6-7B: This is a good stunt versus both run and pass. Rover is playing base technique versus run and covering the near back versus pass. Nose is slanting strong, whip is blitzing the weak A gap, and blood is blitzing the weak B gap.

Diagram 6-7C: This is a good stunt versus pass. Nose is slanting weak, whip is blitzing the strong A gap, and blood is blitzing the weak B gap. Rover is playing base technique versus run and covering the near back versus pass.

Diagram 6-7D: This is a good stunt versus both run and pass. Nose is slanting weak, blood is blitzing the strong A gap, and whip is blitzing the weak B gap. Rover is playing base technique versus run and covering the near back versus pass.

Diagram 6-7E: This is a good stunt versus pass. The strong tackle and nose are slanting strong, and blood is blitzing through the weak A gap. Whip and the weak end are twisting. Rover is playing base technique versus run and covering the near back versus pass.

Diagram 6-7F: This is a good stunt versus pass but weak against run. Nose and the strong tackle are slanting weak, and whip is blitzing through the strong B gap. The weak end and blood are twisting, and rover is playing base technique versus run and covering the near back versus pass.

Diagram 6-7G: This stunt is good versus pass. Nose is slanting weak, and whip is creeping toward the line during cadence and blitzing through the B gap (quick penetration is imperative). The weak end is looping behind whip into the weak A gap. Blood is scraping outside, securing the C gap, and containing the quarterback.

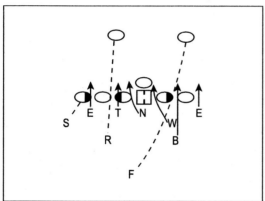

Diagram 6-7b

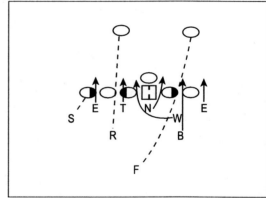

Diagram 6-7c

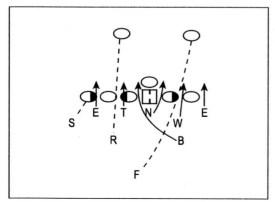

Diagram 6-7d

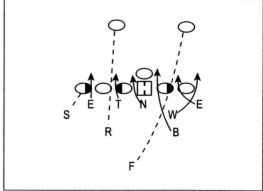

Diagram 6-7e

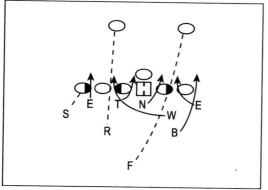

Diagram 6-7f

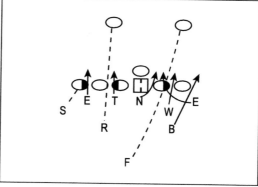

Diagram 6-7g

Z-S Flash Coverage

When confronted by an aceback set, all Z-S flash stunts (Diagram 6-8A) will use the rover as the adjuster. Therefore, any Z-S flash stunt that doesn't send the rover does not need to be checked off versus an aceback set.

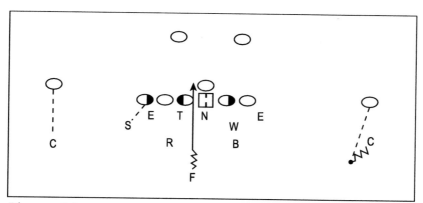

Diagram 6-8a

Z-S Flash Stunts

Diagram 6-8B: This is a good stunt versus pass but weak against run. Rover and blood are playing base technique versus run and covering the near back versus pass. The free safety is blitzing the weak A gap, nose is slanting strong, and whip is creeping toward the line during cadence and blitzing the weak B gap.

Diagram 6-8C: This is a good stunt versus pass. The free safety is blitzing the strong A gap and blood is blitzing the weak A gap. Nose is attacking the center and preventing the center from blocking either the free safety or blood. Whip is creeping toward the line, drawing the guard's block, securing the B gap versus run, and spying the near back versus pass. Rover is playing base technique versus run and covering the near back versus pass.

Diagram 6-8D: This is a good stunt versus pass. Rover is creeping toward the line during cadence and drawing the tackle's block. Versus run, rover is securing the B gap, and spying the near back versus pass. Nose and the strong tackle are slanting weak, and the free safety is blitzing the strong B gap. Whip and the weak end are twisting, and blood is playing base technique versus run and covering the near back versus pass.

Diagram 6-8E: This is a good stunt versus pass and run. The strong end is slanting across the tight end's face, securing the D gap versus run and spying the near back versus pass. Rover is blitzing through the C gap, securing this gap versus run and containing the quarterback versus pass. Nose is slanting weak, and the free safety is blitzing the strong A gap. Blood is playing base technique versus run and delay blitzing behind the free safety versus pass. Whip is creeping toward the line during cadence, securing the B gap versus run, and spying the near back versus pass.

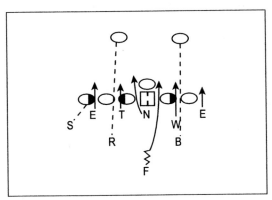

Diagram 6-8b

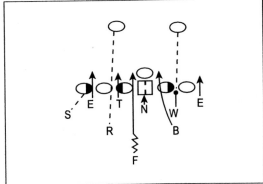

Diagram 6-8c

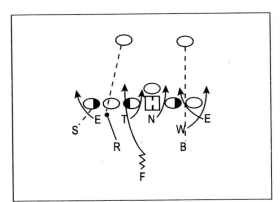

Diagram 6-8d

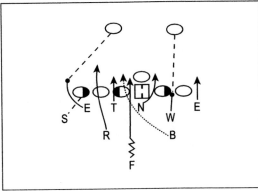

Diagram 6-8e

7

Zoning a Pass Offense with Cover 3

Strengths of a Zone Coverage

- Because defensive backs are keying quarterback (along with the receivers), they can break on the quarterback's throw, which often results in more interceptions.

- Defensive backs are seldom "isolated on an island." Another defender is usually providing help.

- It is usually more difficult for the offense to create a mismatch.

- The defense is less likely to give up the big play while in a zone coverage.

- It is much more difficult for the offense to create "rubs" (a legal version of the old "pick" play).

- If the quarterback is accustomed to seeing mostly man coverage, it may surprise him; furthermore, it may disrupt his play calling.

Weaknesses of a Zone Coverage

- Horizontal seams occur between each zone.

- Each zone can be high-lowed (vertically stretched) by putting one receiver at the bottom of the zone and another one at the top.

- Linebackers can be prevented from dropping to their assigned zone or momentarily frozen with run-action fakes.

- Most zone defenses feature a four-man pass rush, which is usually predictable, and frequently does not exert enough pressure on the quarterback.

- Many zone coverages do not collision pass routes and disrupt the timing between the quarterback and his receivers.

This book's version of cover 3 is different from most other versions because it covers the #1 receiver into the boundary man-man. The boundary corner will, however, receive help (both underneath and over the top) in covering this receiver. When cover 3 is called, the nose will play a weak 1 technique. This change will alter whip's responsibility slightly. Whip will continue to fill the B gap when confronted by weak flow, but against strong flow, whip is responsible for plugging the strongside A gap (Diagram 7-1).

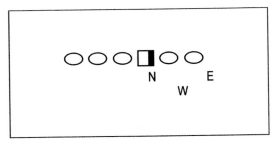

Diagram 7-1a

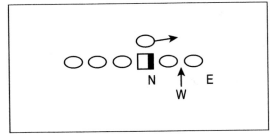

Diagram 7-1b

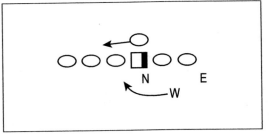

Diagram 7-1c

Zone Drop Pattern Reads

It is very important not only to have a defender drop to a spot on the field, but also to give him specific keys and have him read and react to both the quarterback and his specific keys. The following pattern read guidelines (versus a standard pro formation) will assist defenders who are dropping into one of the cover 3 zones.

Strong Hook-Curl Drop

Drop to a depth of 12 to 15 yards into the strong hook zone. Key #2 (the tight end). If #2 runs a vertical route, stay in the hook and collision him. If #2 releases into the flats, sprint to the curl and look for #1 (the flanker) to run a curl or a post. If #2 runs inside and across your face, try to collision him, and then look for another receiver to run a crossing route into your zone.

Weak Hook-Curl Drop

Open up and drop to a depth of 12 to 15 yards into the weak hook zone. Key #2 (the weakside halfback). If #2 runs a vertical route, stay in the hook and collision him. If #2 releases into the flats, sprint to the curl and look for #1 (the split end) to run a curl or a post. If #2 runs inside and across your face, try to collision him and then look for another receiver to run a crossing route into your zone.

Strong Curl-Out Drop

Open up and drop to a depth of 10 to 12 yards. Your aiming point is three yards inside of where #1 (the flanker) lined up. Key #1. If #1 runs an out, try to get into the throwing lane and get a piece of the ball. If #1 runs a curl or a post, stay inside of his pattern and check #2 (the tight end). If #2 runs an out, you must release from #1's curl or post when #2 crosses your face. If #1 runs a vertical route, sink and check #2 and #3.

Weak Curl-Out Drop

Open up and drop to a depth of 10 to 12 yards. Your aiming point is three yards inside of where #1 (the split end) lined up. Key #1. If #1 runs an out, try to get into the throwing lane and get a piece of the ball. If #1 runs a curl or a post, stay inside of his pattern and check #2 (the weakside halfback). If #2 runs an out, you must release from #1's curl or post when #2 crosses your face. If #1 runs a vertical route, sink and check #2.

Deep Outside 1/3 Drop

See both #1 and #2 as you backpedal. Stay as deep as the deepest receiver in your zone. If #1 runs a short or intermediate route, look for #2 to threaten you deep. If #2 also runs a short or intermediate route, control the speed of your backpedal so that you can break on the ball. If #1 runs a vertical route, maintain a cushion of three to four yards. If #1 runs a post, stay on his outside hip and maintain a sufficient cushion.

Deep Middle 1/3 Drop

Drop midway between the two cornerbacks, stay as deep as the deepest receiver, and play center field. Key #2's release. If it is vertical, you must get into a position to cover it. If #2's route is short, check the split end and flanker for the post.

Two Methods of Zoning Two-Back Sets

Two-back formations can be defended using two different methods. The first method is illustrated in Diagram 7-2. Please note both the similarities and differences between these alignments and those of base cover 1.

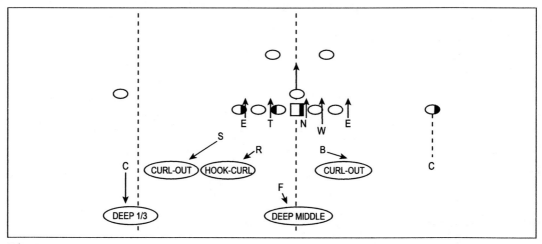

Diagram 7-2a

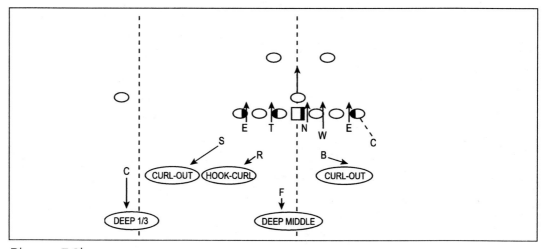

Diagram 7-2b

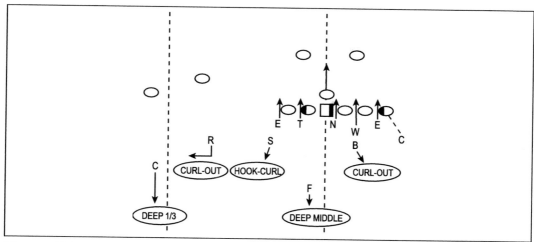

Diagram 7-2c

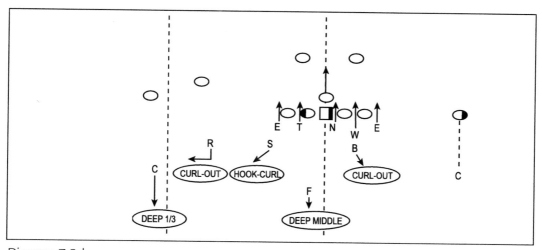

Diagram 7-2d

In this first method, whip aligns into the boundary (or away from the strength of the offensive formation if the ball is in the middle of the field). Whip also blitzes and only three defenders drop into the under-coverage. Three different schemes are employed when whip blitzes (Diagram 7-3). These three stunts can either be executed at the snap of the ball or used as delayed reactions to pass.

The obvious advantage of this first method of playing cover 3 is that it gives you a five-man pass rush. The disadvantage is that it doesn't account for #3 strong (the strong halfback). Traditionally, cover 3 teams drop only two defenders to cover the three strongside zones (hook, curl, out). This tendency is probably one of the reasons that cover 2 was invented. To remedy this problem, you can use a second method (Diagram 7-4) of playing cover 3 versus two-back offensive sets.

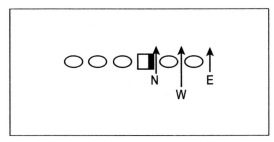

Diagram 7-3a

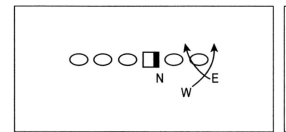

Diagram 7-3b

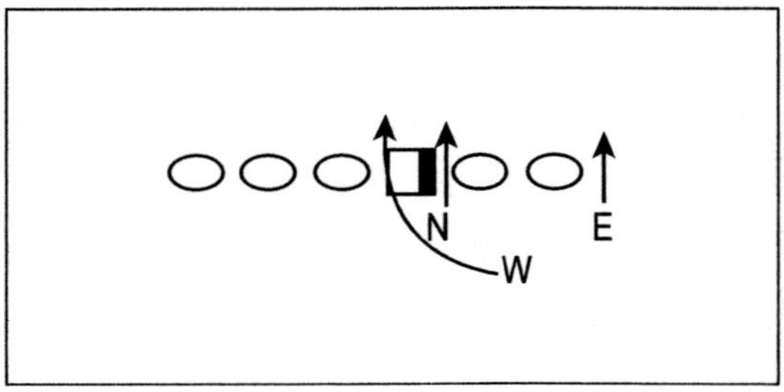

Diagram 7-3c

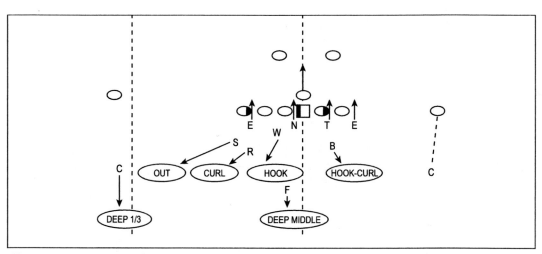

Diagram 7-4a

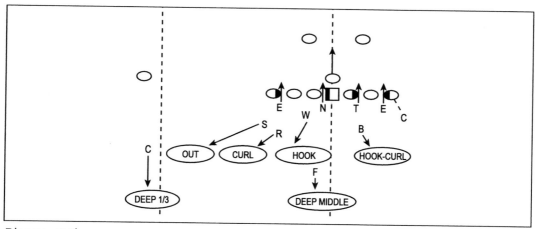

Diagram 7-4b

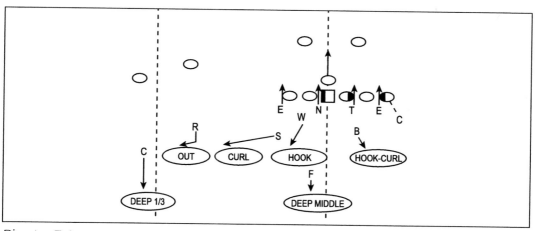

Diagram 7-4c

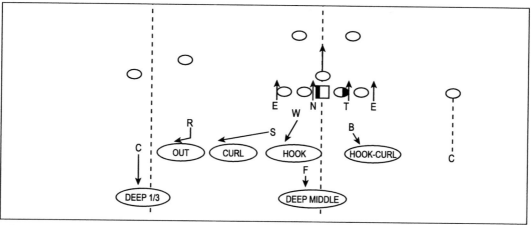

Diagram 7-4d

When this second method is employed, the whip will always align toward the wide side of the field (or toward the strength of the offensive formation if the ball is in the center of the field). This method affords you the luxury of having three defenders dropping into the under-coverage toward the wide side of the field. It also enables you to adequately account for the strongside halfback. The disadvantage of this second method is that it only gives you a four-man pass rush.

Adjusting Cover 3 to Aceback Sets

When confronted by an aceback formation (doubles or trips), you should always align whip into the boundary and drop him into coverage. Diagram 7-5 illustrates the cover 3 assignments and adjustments versus four variations of doubles, and Diagram 7-6 illustrates cover 3 assignments and adjustments versus four variations of trips.

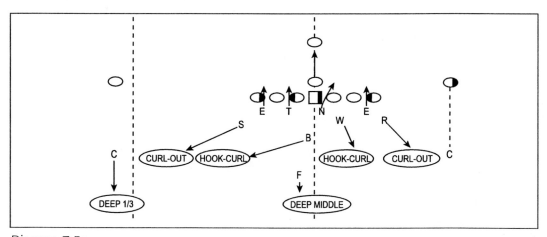

Diagram 7-5a

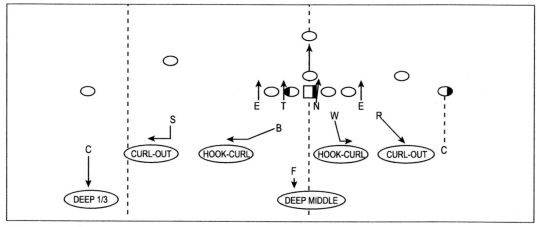

Diagram 7-5b

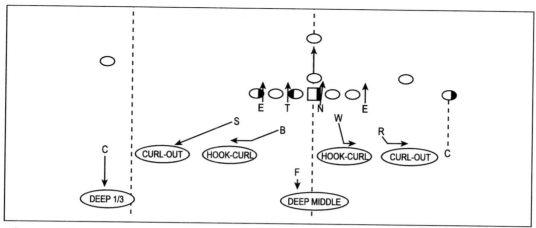

Diagram 7-5c

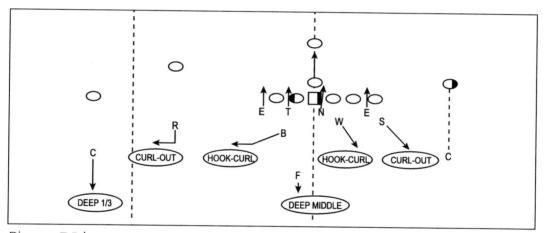

Diagram 7-5d

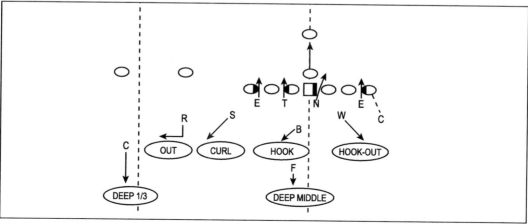

Diagram 7-6a

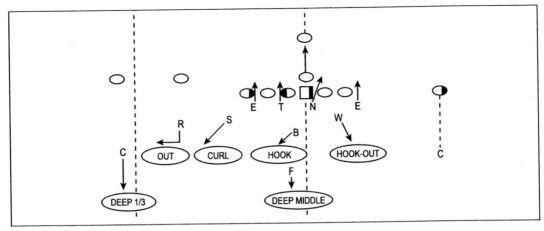

Diagram 7-6b

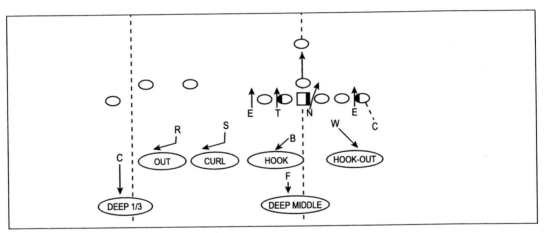

Diagram 7-6c

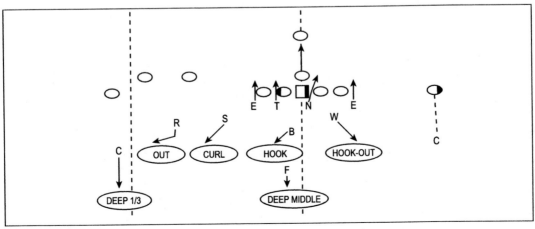

Diagram 7-6d

8

Variations of the Double Eagle Flex

This chapter will introduce four strongside variations, four weakside variations, and three other variations that will affect the entire defensive front. Each strongside variation will be assigned a two-digit number. Each weakside variation is given a one-digit number, and the other variations are given word designations. This numbering/word system enables a coach to create 44 variations of the double eagle flex. At the end of this chapter is a detailed explanation of the assignments, responsibilities, and techniques necessary to teach any variations that differ from the base.

Strongside Variations

70

70 gets its name because the strong end is aligned in a 7 technique. 70 is the base strongside variation, and it has already been explained in detail (Diagram 8-1).

80

80 gets its name because the strong end is aligned in a crash 8 technique. This variation is a good one to use on an obvious passing down. The pressure that the strong end can exert from the edge can often cause protection problems for the

offense. The strong safety will align in a 7 technique and employ the same reads and techniques as the strong end would in the same alignment. Most strong safeties probably won't have the strength to employ this technique against strong running teams (Diagram 8-2).

Diagram 8-1

Diagram 8-2

50

50 gets its name because the strong end is aligned in a 5 technique. This variation is a good change of pace against an offense with a strong inside running game. It can also burden teams that want to employ a fold blocking scheme in an attempt to exploit the strong tackle's 3 technique. It is also an effective deterrent versus (strongside) midline option. The technique is particularly effective when used in conjunction with a variation of 1 rover or zero coverage (Diagram 8-3).

90

90 is the second variation in which the strong end lines up in a 7 technique. It is an excellent variation to use against a good tight end. Because he is being attacked simultaneously by two defenders, the tight end will have a difficult time releasing for passes, blocking the 7 technique, or attempting to release to the second level and block the rover. It is also a good alignment for strong safeties who are experiencing difficulty reading and reacting to their keys (Diagram 8-4).

Diagram 8-3

Diagram 8-4

Weakside Variations

0 Alignment

The 0 alignment gets its name because the nose is aligned in a 0 technique. This is the base weakside variation, and it has already been explained in detail (Diagram 8-5).

1 Alignment

The 1 alignment gets its name because the nose is aligned in a 1 technique. Many double eagle flex teams use 1 as their base weakside variation. The 0 technique is the preferred base because it enables the nose to easily slant into either A gap, making the defense less predictable and enabling you to exploit an offensive tendency. Some teams tilt their nose when employing a 1 alignment, which often causes a center difficulty. The 1 alignment is generally used as a change of pace (Diagram 8-6).

Diagram 8-5

Diagram 8-6

2 Alignment

The 2 alignment gets its name because the nose is aligned in a 2 technique. No detailed explanation of this alignment is given at the end of the chapter because reading from the 2 alignment is not recommended. It is preferable to stunt, slant, and twist out of 2. Diagram 8-8 illustrates six things that you can do out of 2 (Diagram 8-7).

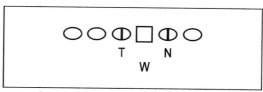

Diagram 8-7

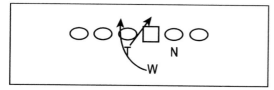

Diagram 8-8a

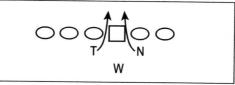

Diagram 8-8b

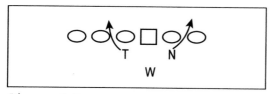

Diagram 8-8c

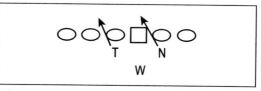

Diagram 8-8d

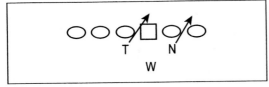

Diagram 8-8e   Diagram 8-8f

3 Alignment

The 3 alignment is the second variation in which the nose is aligned in a 1. Not only does this variation enable you to blitz whip from the edge, it enables you to drop whip into the flats. This variation is also troublesome for aceback teams that want to run the speed option weak. When employing this technique, the whip will basically employ the same reads and techniques as the strong safety would from an 8 alignment (Diagram 8-9).

Diagram 8-9

Other Variations

0 Switch

This variation tells the strong tackle and whip to switch the side of the formation in which they normally align. It is a good change-of-pace alignment. (Diagram 8-10)

1 Switch

This variation tells the strong tackle, nose, and whip to switch the side of the formation in which they normally align. It is also a good change-of-pace alignment (Diagram 8-11).

Diagram 8-10   Diagram 8-11

X

This variation enables you to put nine defenders in the box versus a two-back formation. It is extremely effective versus strong running games and solves many of the problems that an unbalanced eight-man front such as the double eagle flex may experience against the option (Diagram 8-12).

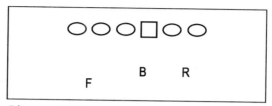

Diagram 8-12

44 Variations of the Double Eagle Flex

Diagram 8-13 illustrates 16 variations of the base (70) alignment that can be created with the numbering/name system that has just been described. If you were to pencil out all of the possibilities, you would find 44 total possibilities. The remainder of this chapter will explain in detail all of the techniques and responsibilities of the variations presented in this chapter.

1 Technique-Nose

Stance and Alignment: Defender lines up with his inside eye aligned on the outside eye of the center (1 technique) in a three- or four-point stance with a slight stagger of his inside foot.

Responsibilities:

- Run Toward: Weakside A gap.
- Run Away: Squeeze strongside A gap.
- Pass: Rush weakside A gap.

Keys:

- Primary: Center, ball movement.
- Secondary: Weakside guard.

Important Techniques/Concepts: Defender's target is the center's outside eye. He will employ a crush technique by attacking the center with his hands (inside lockout). He

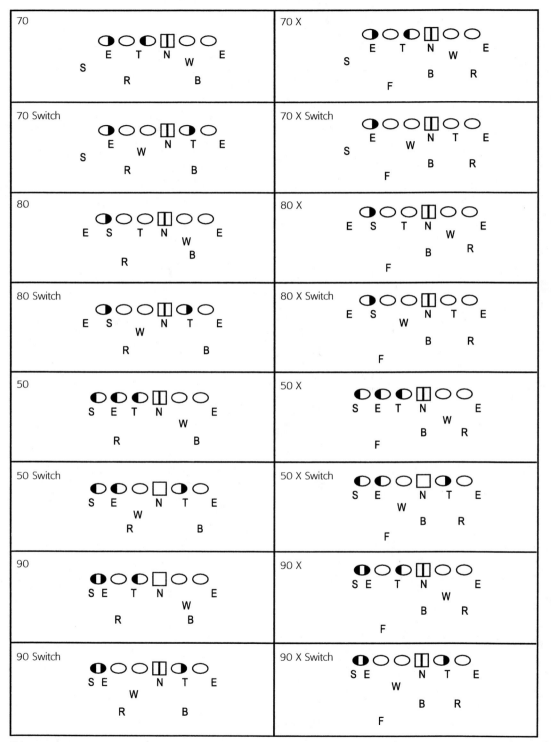

Diagram 8-13

will keep his shoulders square. It is important that he recognizes that a pulling guard indicates point of attack.

Key Blocks:

- Center drive block: Defender must knock center back, stay square, and locate the ball.
- Guard/center double-team: Defender must attack the guard, stay low, and not get driven back. As a last resort, defender will drop his outside hip and plug the A gap by rolling outside.
- Center hook block: Defender must control center's outside shoulder, keep his own shoulders parallel, and plug the A gap. He can't get hooked.
- Weak zone: Defender will play it like a center hook block and control the center's outside shoulder.
- Strong zone: Defender will jam the center, prevent the center from releasing to the second level, and then control the guard's outside shoulder.
- Center blocks strong/down block by guard: Defender will release pressure from the center and control the outside shoulder of the guard. He will work across the guard's face and pursue the ball from an inside-out position.
- Guard pulls strong/cut-off: Defender should beat center's block, penetrate across the line of scrimmage, and follow the guard to the point of attack. If defender is unable to penetrate, he should flatten across center's face and pursue the ball from an inside-out position.
- Pass: Defender will rush weakside A gap.

5 Technique-Strong End

Stance and Alignment: Three- or four-point stance, inside foot back. 5 technique: player's inside foot should split the offensive tackle's stance.

Responsibilities:

- Run Toward: C gap.
- Run Away: Squeeze B.
- Pass: Contain quarterback.

Keys:

- Primary: Tackle, ball movement.
- Secondary: Tight end, near back, pulling linemen.

Important Techniques/Concepts: Defender's target is the guard's outside shoulder. His first step is with his inside foot. He must maintain outside leverage, secure the C gap, and not get hooked by the tackle.

Key Blocks:

- Tackle drive block: Defender must read tackle's head, fight pressure, and secure the C gap before pursuing the ball.

- Tackle hook block: Defender must maintain outside leverage, keep his shoulders parallel to the line of scrimmage, and plug the C gap.

- Tackle turnout block: Defender must squeeze the B gap with the tackle's body and look for cutback as he pursues down the line.

- Tackle/tight end double-team: Defender must attack the tight end and not get driven back. As a last resort, he should drop his outside hip and roll into and plug the C gap.

- Strong zone: Defender must play the tackle's block like a hook block.

- Tackle blocks inside/tight end cracks: Defender must first jam the tackle, release pressure, and then flatten across tight end's face.

- Tackle blocks inside/no outside pressure: This is a trap, or a guard/tackle crossblock. Defender must immediately squeeze the B gap and attack whoever blocks him with an outside forearm. He must spill the play outside.

- Tackle pulls inside: This is most likely a counter trey. Defender must get in the tackle's hip pocket and follow him to the point of attack.

- Tackle pulls outside: If the tight end cracks on the defender, he must fight outside pressure and flatten across the tight end's face. If the tight end doesn't crack, the play is either a quick pitch or a trap. The defender must read the backfield action and trap the trapper (if the play is a trap) or pursue the quick pitch flat down the line. If the defender attempts to stop a quick pitch with penetration across the line, he will end up chasing air.

- Tackle pass blocks: Defender must contain the quarterback.

9 Technique-Strong Safety

Stance and Alignment: Two-point stance. Feet parallel or slight stagger of inside foot. 9 technique: defender's inside foot is slightly inside of tight end's outside foot.

Responsibilities:

- Run Toward: D gap.
- Run Away: Depends upon stunt and coverage.

- Pass: Depends upon stunt and coverage.

Keys:

- Primary: Tight end.
- Secondary: Near back, pulling linemen, the ball.

Important Techniques: Defender must step with inside foot and jam the tight end. He must maintain outside leverage and not get driven back or hooked. He will attack the tight end with his hands and use a forearm rip when taking on a running back or pulling lineman. When dealing with a cut block, the defender must use his hands, sprawl, and immediately ricochet off the ground.

Key Blocks:

- Tight end hook block defender: He will immediately get his hands on the tight end and lock him out. He must control the tight end's outside shoulder and secure the D gap.
- Tight end turnout block/strongside run in the B or C gap: Defender will create a stalemate and squeeze the C gap with the tight end's body while maintaining outside leverage on the ball.
- Tight end releases, near back kick-out block: As the defender jams the tight end, he must see the near back out of his periphery. Defender must close back inside and close the C gap. He will attack the blocker with an outside forearm, and spill the play outside. It is important that the defender does not penetrate across the line of scrimmage and create an alley for the ballcarrier.
- Tight end releases, flow away: Depends upon stunt and coverage.
- Tight end blocks inside: Defender must jam the tight end and squeeze the C gap. He will then attack the blocker (near back or pulling lineman) with his outside shoulder and spill the play outside.
- Tight end releases/pass: Depends upon stunt and coverage.

4i Technique-Weak Tackle

Stance and Alignment: Three- or four-point stance, outside foot back. Player will line up on inside shoulder of the offensive tackle.

Responsibilities:

- Run Toward: B gap.
- Run Away: Squeeze A gap.

- Pass: Depends upon coverage and stunt.

Keys:

- Primary: Guard-tackle.
- Secondary: Near back, pulling linemen.

Important Techniques/Concepts: Defender's target is the tackle's inside shoulder. His first step is with his outside foot. He will attack the tackle with a hand shiver. He must maintain inside leverage and secure the B gap.

Key Blocks:

- Tackle drive block: Defender must feel pressure and fight pressure using outside-n leverage.
- Guard blocks inside, no pressure from tackle: This is a trap. Defender must attack the trapper with his outside forearm and spill the play outside.
- Strong zone: Defender will close hard down the line. He will rip through the tackle's head with his outside forearm and pursue the ball from an inside-out position, checking for cutback.
- Weak zone: Defender must first jam the tackle and then attack and control the guard's outside shoulder. Defender will keep his shoulders square to the line as he pursues outside.
- Tackle pass blocks: Depends upon stunt and coverage.

8 Crash Technique-Strong End

Stance and Alignment: Tilted three- or four-point stance, on the line, one to two yards outside of the tight end.

Responsibilities:

- Run Toward: Contain.
- Run Away: Chase.
- Pass: Contain the quarterback.

Keys:

- Primary: Near back.
- Secondary: Ball.

Important Techniques/Concepts: Defender's target is the junction of the near back's neck and shoulders. At the snap, he will crash toward this landmark, maintain outside leverage, and attack all blockers with an inside forearm rip.

Key Blocks:

- Near back kick-out block: Defender will squeeze the play inside. He will attack the blocker with an inside forearm rip and maintain the ability to react outside.

- Near back hook block: Defender will force the play wide and deep. He will attack the blocker with an inside forearm rip, keep the ballcarrier deeper than himself, and then ricochet off the blocker as the ballcarrier bounces the play outside.

- Near back blocks inside: Defender will redirect his course as he mirrors the path of the near back. He will squeeze play inside, maintain outside leverage on the ball, and be prepared for the ballcarrier to bounce outside.

- Tight end kick-out block: Defender will attack the tight end with an inside forearm rip and use the tight end's body to restrict the C gap. He will maintain outside leverage on the ball and expect the play to bounce outside.

- Flow away: Defender will chase the play as deep as the ball. He will check for counter and reverse.

- Near back pass blocks: Defender will contain the quarterback.

9

Dealing with
Forced Assignment Football

A real offense forces a defense to play assignment football. A coach can flimflam any offense that doesn't force his defense to play assignment football with multiple stems, stunts, and fronts. This chapter presents a number of offensive plays that do force assignment football and explains how the double eagle flex deals with these plays.

A Well-Orchestrated Dropback Pass Offense

The following tactics will successfully cause the most problems for this type of offensive attack:

- Disguise coverages and confuse the quarterback's reads.

- Collision receivers and disrupt the timing of pass routes.

- Pressure the quarterback so that he must throw off-balance and make hurried throws and bad decisions.

- Confuse the quarterback's hot reads so that he ends up dumping the ball off to receivers in long passing situations (the zone blitz schemes presented in Chapter 5 will accomplish this objective).

All of these tactics are the essence of the double eagle flex, which is the main reason why this defense was invented to stop the prolific pass offenses that are the trademark of Canadian football.

Shotgun Counter Trey Read

Almost everyone in the country seems to be running some variation of this package (Diagram 9-1). The following points are the keys to stopping this play:

- The free safety's alignment enables him to play center field versus pass and quickly support run.

- Blood and whip will align toward the aceback. Blood will cover the aceback versus pass. Whip will delay blitz the quarterback versus pass. Both blood and whip will read their near guard.

- When the offensive tackle blocks inside, the strong end will run flat down the line of scrimmage and aggressively attack the pulling guard. The strong end's job is to close the C gap and knock the pulling guard backwards into the pulling tackle and thus prevent the tackle from blocking anyone.

- If the strong end does his job, the ballcarrier will be forced to bounce the play outside. The free safety, who is also keying the pulling guard, will immediately fill off the tail of the strong end and contain the ballcarrier as he sees the blocking scheme develop.

- Whip will immediately fast flow and pursue the ball from an inside-out position as he sees the guard pull.

- The weak end, upon seeing the tackle pull, will immediately attack the quarterback.

- Blood will take his two shuffle steps and make certain that the weak end has done his job. When he sees that the quarterback has been accounted for, blood will then work downhill and pursue the ball from an inside-out position.

Shotgun Option

- The alignment of blood pretty much takes this play away from the offense.

- As the weak end sees the tackle block inside, he will play the quarterback. Some coaches will want the end to immediately attack the quarterback. Others may want the end to feather (slow play) the quarterback. No matter which technique is chosen, it is imperative that the end gets his hat on the quarterback's pitch arm as he tackles him.

- Some coaches may also wish to tighten the end so that he can jam the tackle from getting a clean shot at whip. The disadvantage is that a tighter alignment may hinder the end's pass rush.
- Blood will immediately scrape outside and deny the quarterback the pitch.
- The free safety will play the alley and think quarterback-pitch.

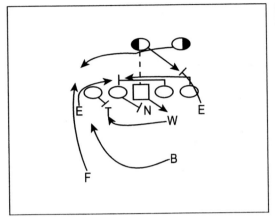 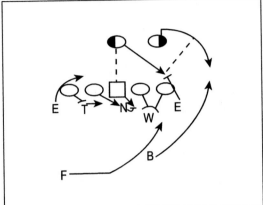

Diagram 9-1. Shotgun counter trey read　　　Diagram 9-2. Shotgun option

An Aceback Strong Speed Option

- This is a very common aceback play. Its purpose is to try to force an inside linebacker in a reduced eight-man front to cover the pitch. The manner in which the free safety is played defeats this purpose.
- Hopefully, the strong end will be able to help tackle the quarterback. At worst, the strong end should be able to force the quarterback to run uphill.
- The strong safety is the primary player responsible for tackling the quarterback (quick force or feather).
- Upon reading this play, the free safety will immediately scrape outside and take away the pitch.
- The strongside offensive tackle will have a free shot at sealing off the second level but he will have to contend with two players (blood and whip). This factor is one of the major advantages of a four-level defense.
- If the offense has a good play-action pass off this action, a coach may want to consider taking the players who normally funnel receivers into the free safety and having them play an inside leverage technique and abandon the funnel.

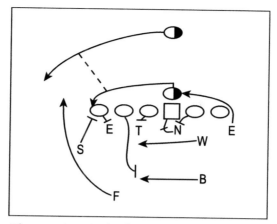

Diagram 9-3. Aceback strong speed option

Weakside Veer

- 70 X is a great front versus both the weakside and strongside veer.

- A coach can defense this play in two ways, and both have merit. A coach has the option of choosing only one method or using both.

- The first option is illustrated in Diagram 9-4A. When the weak end sees the tackle block inside, he will tackle first show (the dive). He will attempt to tackle the dive back as deep in the backfield as possible in an attempt to force the quarterback to run uphill. Blood is responsible for tackling the quarterback and rover will scrape to the pitch. The free safety will take two lateral shuffle steps and fill the alley.

- The second strategy (Diagram 9-4B) is to have the end attack the mesh point and immediately tackle the quarterback. This action should force the dive back inside. Tackling the dive becomes the joint responsibility of the nose, whip, and blood. Both the rover and free safety's assignments are identical to the first method.

- These same basic principles can be applied to defending the strongside veer.

Midline Option

- 70 X is also a great front versus the midline option (Diagram 9-5).

- The strong tackle should tackle the dive back as deep in the backfield as possible. He should receive considerable help from both whip and rover. Blood will immediately plug the B gap and get a clean shot at the quarterback. The free safety is responsible for scraping outside and tackling the pitch.

- If a coach wishes to play zero coverage, the free safety will guard the tight end and the strong safety can immediately jump the pitch.

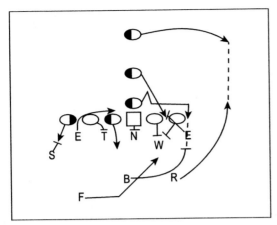
Diagram 9-4a. Weakside veer

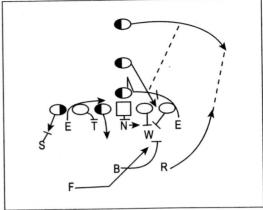
Diagram 9-4b. Weakside veer

Full-Flow Play-Action Pass

- This is a very effective pass versus most eight-man fronts that play a lot of cover 3. It can be run to either the strongside or weakside.

- The reason this play is so successful is that an eight-man front that plays zone leaves their outside linebacker in the awkward dilemma of: "Is the fullback going to block, or is he releasing for a pass?"

- This pass is not effective versus the double eagle flex because blood is responsible for containment and blood must scrape outside in order to contain. Having to scrape outside is what enables blood to easily see the fullback releasing into the flats. He will therefore automatically cover the fullback.

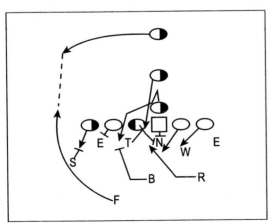
Diagram 9-5. Midline option

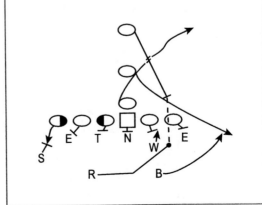
Diagram 9-6. Full-flow play-action pass

Counter Trey Waggle Pass

- This is another effective pass versus almost any type of defense.

- Because blood is keying both the near guard and backfield, it becomes immediately evident to blood that the play is not a counter trey (neither the guard nor tackle are pulling). Blood should therefore not even be fooled into taking any lateral shuffle steps. He should immediately jump the fullback's pattern.

The Wing-T Offense

- Like the option, this offense forces the defense to play assignment football.

- The 90 alignment is effective versus this offense.

- Versus the bootleg pass (1): Whip is assigned the fullback, the strong safety will cover the tight end, the boundary corner will cover the wingback, rover will check for the halfback screen, and the free safety will play center field.

- Versus the bootleg keep (3): The weak end and rover are responsible for containing the quarterback.

- Versus the trap (1): Whip, nose and strong tackle are responsible for stopping this play.

- Versus the buck sweep (2): The 90 alignment's double jam impairs the tight end's down block on the 7 technique. This alignment also immediately puts the strong safety in the paths of the pulling guards. The boundary corner is the primary force. Rover will scrape off the strong corner's tail and the free safety will fill the alley.

- Versus the counter (4): The boundary corner is responsible for alerting the team. Blood and the strong end must contain the play and the free safety must plug the alley.

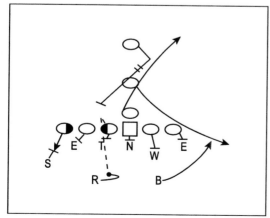

Diagram 9-7. Counter trey waggle pass

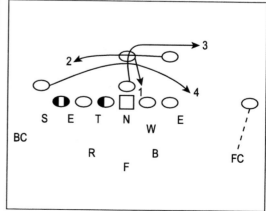

Diagram 9-8. The wing-T offense

The Aceback Cluster Formation

- With the proliferation of man coverage, many teams are getting into the aceback cluster formation in an attempt to create rubs (legal picks).

- This formation is not a real problem for the double eagle flex. Both cover 1 (Diagram 9-9A) and cover 3 (Diagram 9-9B) adapt well to the cluster.

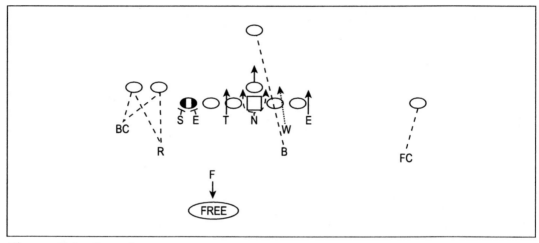

Diagram 9-9a. Cover 1

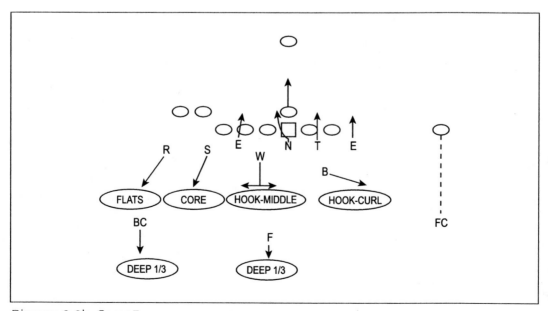

Diagram 9-9b. Cover 3

Cover 1

- The first thing that you want to do is jam the cluster receiver aligned on the line of scrimmage. Diagram 9-9A shows how to use a 90 alignment to get a double jam on the tight end.

- The rover and boundary corner will deal with the next two receivers by employing both a banjo (combo) technique and by playing at different levels.

- The strong safety and blood are both in excellent position to take away the speed option pitch (the strong safety and weak end are responsible for the quarterback keep).

- Versus pass, the free safety is in excellent position to drop over the top of the cluster.

Cover 3

- When zone coverage is employed, you should line up in a 50 switch. This alignment enables you to drop three linebackers toward the cluster and still be sound versus the weakside speed option.

- Rover is aligned on the line of scrimmage and slightly outside of the #1 receiver. From this position, he will be able to drop to the flats or quickly contain strongside run.

- Because rover is able to contain strongside run, the free safety is able to line up in the middle of the formation and drop to center field versus pass and provide alley support to both sides of the formation versus run.

The Empty Formation

- Almost every team now uses some form of the empty formation.

- A number of schools of thought exist on how to defense this offensive tactic, which seems to increase each year in popularity. Some coaches believe that the best defense is to rush three and drop eight; others believe in sending the house. Probably the best tactic will depend upon the down-and-distance situation, the mobility of the quarterback, and how the defensive back's speed and skill match up with that of the wide receivers.

- Diagrams 9-10 through 9-14 illustrate five possible double eagle flex tactics versus the empty formation.

- Diagram 9-10 illustrates a cover 3 that drops eight and rushes three. The big questions that a coach must ask when contemplating this tactic are: "Will the defense be able to stop the quarterback draw (if the quarterback is mobile)?" and "Will the pass rush be adequate to pressure the quarterback?"

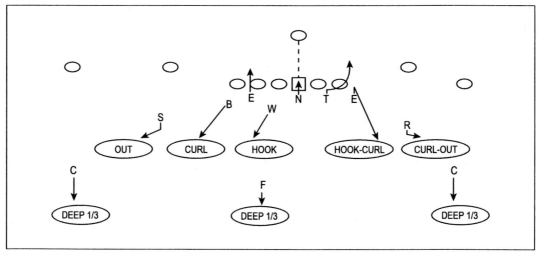

Diagram 9-10.

- Diagram 9-11 illustrates a hybrid version of cover 3 that zones the strength of the formation, but employs man coverage toward the weakside of the formation. This tactic employs a four-man pass rush, which should exert more pressure on the quarterback. When considering this tactic, it is vital to make certain that the field corner and rover are able to cover the two wide receivers. (Note: It is important that both the field corner and rover play an inside leverage technique because the offense will probably try to freeze the free safety with a pattern that will prevent him from providing much help over the top.)

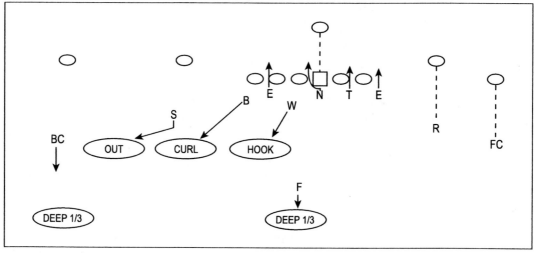

Diagram 9-11.

- Diagram 9-12 illustrates a version of cover 1. This variation will provide the defense with a five-man pass rush that should provide plenty of pressure on the quarterback. Another advantage is that at least three defenders (blood, rover, and the free safety) are jamming receivers and funneling them into the free safety. (If the ball is on the hash, the boundary corner will also be able to employ a jam-and-funnel technique).

- Diagram 9-13 shows the fire zone blitz version of cover 1 versus the empty formation. The darkened pass receivers are the three receivers that will be combo covered by the strong safety, nose, and rover.

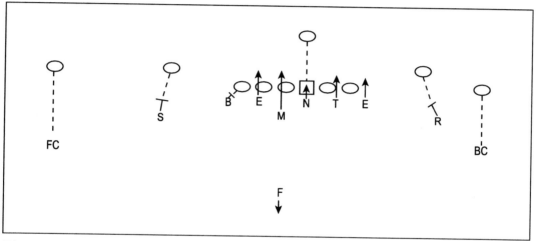

Diagram 9-12.

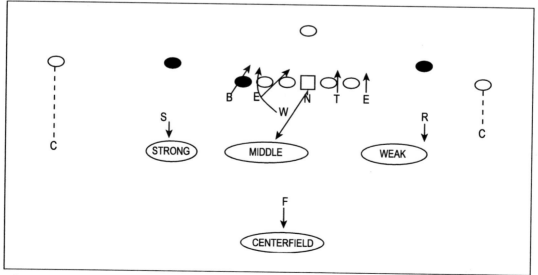

Diagram 9-13.

- The final tactic is illustrated in Diagram 9-14. When this tactic is employed, the defense is truly sending the house—which may result in a very big play for either the offense or the defense.

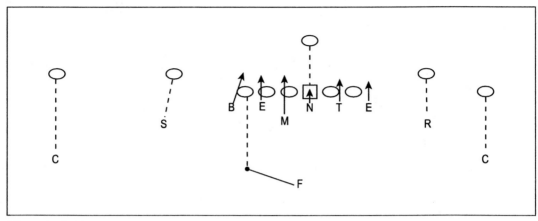

Diagram 9-14.